Counseling in the Family Law System

Virginia B. Allen, EdD, LCPC, NCC, has been a licensed clinical professional counselor (LCPC) in Idaho for 30 years; for 25 of these years she has worked in private practice as a custody evaluator for the magistrate courts. Dr. Allen was one of the original forensic counselors regularly used by the family courts; through her ground-level involvement in her role as an LCPC, she was instrumental in opening the field of forensic counseling to licensed professional counselors in Idaho.

Dr. Allen has performed thousands of custody evaluations, given numerous second opinions, and testified in court hundreds of times. Dr. Allen has also presented many times on the state, regional, and national levels to counselors, psychologists, social workers, attorneys, and judges. She is a member of the Idaho Supreme Court Family and Children in the Courts Committee, which sets family law rules for the Idaho Magistrate Courts.

Dr. Allen is a Professor Emeritus in the Idaho State University Department of Counseling, in which she served as a counselor educator for 30 years.

Counseling in the Family Law System
A Professional Counselor's Guide

Virginia B. Allen, EdD, LCPC, NCC

SPRINGER PUBLISHING COMPANY
NEW YORK

Springer Publishing Company, LLC
11 West 42nd Street
New York, NY 10036
www.springerpub.com

Acquisitions Editor: Nancy S. Hale
Production Editor: Shelby Peak
Composition: Amnet

ISBN: 978-0-8261-9829-7
e-book ISBN: 978-0-8261-9835-8

14 15 16 17 / 5 4 3 2 1

The author and the publisher of this Work have made every effort to use sources believed to be reliable to provide information that is accurate and compatible with the standards generally accepted at the time of publication. The author and publisher shall not be liable for any special, consequential, or exemplary damages resulting, in whole or in part, from the readers' use of, or reliance on, the information contained in this book. The publisher has no responsibility for the persistence or accuracy of URLs for external or third-party Internet websites referred to in this publication and does not guarantee that any content on such websites is, or will remain, accurate or appropriate.

Library of Congress Cataloging-in-Publication Data

Allen, Virginia B.
  Counseling in the family law system : a professional counselor's guide /
Virginia B. Allen, ED.D, LCPC, NCC.
    pages cm
  Includes bibliographical references.
  ISBN 978-0-8261-9829-7 (print : alk. paper) — ISBN 978-0-8261-9835-8 (e-book)
  1. Counseling—Handbooks, manuals, etc. 2. Criminal psychology. 3. Criminal behavior—Prevention.
I. Title.
  BF636.6.A45 2014
  346.7301'50269—dc23   2014008108

Printed in the United States of America by Gasch Printing.

CONTENTS

FOREWORD

I am an attorney. I have practiced more than 45 years, mostly litigating family law. And I know that courtrooms are filled with fear: The judge fears making a reversible ruling. The attorneys fear losing the case. The client fears what the judge may do with the most precious and vulnerable people in that client's life. It is into this nightmare of uncertainty, anxiety, sobs, and fear that a custody evaluator goes. By giving the trial judge information that helps the court reach its decision, the evaluator affects the outcome of a case as well as its players.

In my years litigating family law, it is an understatement to say that I was careful in selecting an expert witness. I looked for

- Someone who analyzed not only the case's custody issues, but also the dynamics between parents and other family members involved in the case
- Someone who told me what I needed to hear, not what I wanted to hear
- Someone who presented well to my clients, to the court, and to the opposition
- Someone whose quick mind and firm grasp of the material helped him or her anticipate the next question in a cross-examination
- Someone whose communication skills allowed him or her to explain a sophisticated, difficult issue and its resolution to someone with a junior high school education
- Someone who did not leave the impression that he or she was teaching or talking down to the judge or the opposing counsel
- Someone who knew that family law cases are not about winning, but rather about helping those involved

Since 1980, for me, that person has primarily been Dr. Virginia Allen. As my forensic expert, she has served many roles in my family law cases—and not always in the courtroom. I asked her advice about cases, including their parties, clients, and dynamics, even when I didn't use her in court. I asked her to help counsel my clients about what the future held in cases of divorce. Occasionally, I asked her to attend a deposition of an opposing expert with me to help me frame questions and evaluate the opposing expert and his or her credibility and credentials. Thus, Dr. Allen's involvement did not end with the forensic service she provided me, judges, and other attorneys.

Indeed, Dr. Allen also stood at the forefront in helping effect dramatic changes in Idaho family law. In about 1995, I served as member of the Idaho Bench/Bar Committee to Protect Children of High Conflict Divorce, which served to formulate recommendations for judges dealing with high-conflict divorce affecting Idaho children. Dr. Allen served on several local 6th District Court committees that helped develop those recommendations. When I became co-chair of the State Children and Family in the Courts Committee, I asked her to serve as its mental health professional. Dr. Allen was foundational in her attempts to encourage others to see the value of evaluators, mediators, case managers, and parenting coordinators to high-conflict cases. Much of these are commonplace today in Idaho family law cases, but were decidedly not at the time of the Idaho Bench/Bar's 1996 recommendations. Most recently, Dr. Allen provided thoughtful input regarding the State Committee's work on Idaho's first child custody evaluation rule, which sets the standards governing both who may perform custody evaluations and the nature of those evaluations.

Thus, Dr. Allen has been involved in the family courts for many years: not only in the courtroom, but also in legal offices, in judicial chambers, and in court committees. She is a true expert, someone who has lived custody evaluation. She has seen and spoken with children and their parents. She knows how to present her evaluations in a courtroom credibly. And she brings all that expertise, knowledge, and experience to this book. She bases her expertise on years spent teaching in a college setting, performing numerous evaluations, and spending countless hours in courtrooms. And she knows that knowledge and preparation are the best tools with which to displace courtroom anxiety.

If you want to be involved in family law counseling in the family court system, then I encourage you to read and use this book. For those of you wondering whether to become an evaluator, this book will help you if you want to work in the family court system. Take heart: You can indeed acquire the training, education, and skills needed for involvement in the family courts.

And for those of you who are evaluators, this book can help you improve and perfect your skills. To become an accepted expert contributing something meaningful to the family law system, preparation, preparation, and more preparation is essential. Preparation provides you with the knowledge and expertise to make the contribution you desire. And it all starts here, in this text.

I encourage you to be involved. I encourage you to participate in this difficult but rewarding field of work. And I hope you make a difference. If this book helps you reach out and minimize the pain of a single child or family struggling in the Idaho family court system, then your forensic career is a success. And, like Dr. Allen, you will have made a difference. Good luck!

Thomas F. Dial, JD

ACKNOWLEDGMENTS

I want to thank the Idaho magistrate judges and the family law attorneys in Idaho for giving me the opportunity of working with them as a custody evaluator all these many years. Not only did I enjoy working with each one of you, but I also learned from each one of you.

I also want to thank the families who came to my office, who told me their stories and who shared their lives with me during one of the most difficult times a family can face.

My heartfelt thanks goes to Tom Dial for his time and the kind words he wrote about me. I can assure Tom that it is always my pleasure to work with him.

I give high praise to the editors of this book. Their professionalism, patience, and good humor made this book look as good as it does.

Finally, I also thank my children, my husband, and my friends for encouraging me to write this book. At least now I can say I have written a book.

1

What Is Forensic Counseling?

Welcome to the world of forensic counseling. Forensics has been around a long time. Other professions, particularly criminal justice, psychology, and psychiatry, have had their fingers in the forensic pie for many years. But counseling is just now recognizing that this area of expertise is a natural fit for professional counselors. Forensics relies on relationship-building, active listening, reflection, confrontation, hypothesis, and deduction. It uses all the skills of a professional counselor and then makes additional demands in the forms of relationships with clients, attorneys, and judges. Forensic counseling covers a broad spectrum: from counseling with juvenile delinquents and prisoners to working with pathologists, forensic examiners, and law enforcement officers. But before narrowing the scope of forensics for the purpose of this book, it is best that we start at the beginning to understand how the field of forensics has evolved into what it means today for professional counselors.

Forensics is the process of relating or dealing with the application of scientific knowledge to legal problems. In other words, forensics uses knowledge (both objective and subjective) to better understand facts and circumstances for the purpose of clarifying legal issues. Forensics uses professional knowledge and expertise to isolate understandable and usable information about a case's issues to help make reasonable recommendations for resolving that case. For the professional counselor, this means using specific expertise, knowledge, and practice to help others understand pertinent information that can help resolve conflicts; this includes making recommendations that can help attorneys, judges, parents, and children continue their lives in a positive, growth-producing manner.

To better understand forensics, you have to step back in time. In 1248, in China, forensic science was used to identify a sickle and thereby a murderer. But not until the 16th century did European medical practitioners begin systematically gathering information about causes and manners of death. This expanded to identification of poisons in the bodies of homicide victims, then to systematic studies of how different diseases cause specific changes in human organs. These scientific studies allowed the use of forensics in criminal cases to prove (or disprove) guilt. As a case in point, the uses of logic and procedure in a criminal investigation are generally traced back to the case of John Toms, who in 1784 was tried and convicted of murdering Edward Culshaw using a pistol. Culshaw's body was examined and the pistol wad removed from the pistol. It was determined that the paper of the pistol wad matched perfectly the torn newspaper found in Tom's pocket: evidence gathered through forensic inquiry at its best.

SCIENTIFIC FORENSICS

Over many years, the use of forensic science in criminal investigation expanded. New forensic scientific methods were introduced and established by British pathologists such as Bernard Spilsbury, Francis Camps, Sydney Smith, and Keith Simpson; in 1909, the first school of forensic science was founded in Great Britain by Rodolphe Reiss. The growth of forensic science continued through publications and methods introduced around the world. An increasing number of forensic scientists became involved in criminal investigations, using formal procedures to provide evidence used in convictions and acquittals.

Numerous national forensic science professional organizations now exist that focus on the use of forensic science in criminal investigations, including the American Academy of Forensic Sciences (1948), the Canadian Society of Forensic Science (1953), the British Academy of Forensic Sciences (1960), and the Australian Academy of Forensic Sciences (1967). The members of these professional organizations publish articles and work professionally in forensic science. With the aid of these professional societies, and through the advances and changes in technologies and cultures, including mores and societal expectations, the scope of forensic science has continued to expand.

From a scientific standpoint, the field now includes sophisticated methodologies such as DNA evidence, trace evidence, body decomposition, impression evidence (e.g., fingerprints, tire tracks, footwear impressions), controlled substances (both legal and illegal), ballistics, firearm marks, and weapon and tool marks. Databanks available worldwide now allow the comparison of information gathered at various crime scenes, greatly aiding forensic scientists.

Technological progress has required the development of the area of investigation often called *computational forensics*, which includes tracking digital communications and wire transfers as well as developing algorithms and software. Additionally, *digital forensics* is the use of scientific techniques to recover data from electronic and digital media. In addition, modern forensics delves into the investigation of accounting evidence. Even forensic anthropology has been enhanced by new technologies aiding the recovery and identification of bodies and skeletal remains.

The list of forensic specialties goes on and on and continues to expand as different needs arise in the criminal world of investigation. Some of the more interesting subspecialties include forensic botany (the study of plant life), forensic dactyloscopy (the study of fingerprints), forensic entomology (the study of insects around or in bodies to determine time of death or movement of the body), forensic limnology (the study of evidence collected around fresh water sources), forensic odontology (the study of teeth), and forensic psychiatry (the study of criminology and human behavior). And many more subspecialties exist, all of them making for good books, television shows, and movies. Forensic science has certainly been instrumental in providing evidence in criminal cases—but it is also fodder for great entertainment.

Popular culture has embraced the field of forensics and all the suspense it can provide. Sherlock Holmes, Sir Arthur Conan Doyle's famous fictional private detective, relied heavily on forensic science in his investigations. Agatha Christie's Hercule Poirot and Miss Marple were also users—and where would Dick Tracy be without it? Perry Mason brought the world of forensic science into the living rooms of millions of people through that television series; indeed, entire television series are predicated on forensic investigation. Consider *Quincy, M.E.*, the entire premise of which was police work and the world of forensic medicine. And today a wide range of television series have forensic investigation at their core: *CSI, The Mentalist, Elementary, Law and Order, Body of Proof*—the list goes on. Forensic science has also spawned nonfiction shows, such as *Forensic Files*, that introduce the public to the world of forensic investigation. Movies have also gotten into the act, with productions that include *Sherlock Holmes, Broken City*, and the *Die Hard* movies.

All these opportunities to watch actors use forensic science to solve crimes, however, have misled the public into believing that nearly all cases can be solved using forensics and (worse) that forensic science is always correct. In reality, forensic science cannot always solve crimes, cannot always provide the crucial information in under an hour, and simply is not always correct. It is important to remember this core admission, because that simple concept earned a Supreme Court ruling: Any forensic investigator must be able to testify in court and be cross-examined in court about his or her conclusions. The *Melendez–Diaz* Supreme Court ruling pointed out that a document is not susceptible to cross-examination: Only the author of the report can be cross-examined. Accordingly, no report can be allowed to speak for itself: Its preparer must be brought before the bench on request. This recent decision affects the conclusions developed by many types of forensics workers who prepare reports to assist the court. We now move from the more scientific investigations of forensics to the area of forensics that employs mental health professionals, including psychiatrists, psychologists, social workers, and professional counselors.

FORENSICS USED BY MENTAL HEALTH PROVIDERS

As has happened in the past, psychiatry and psychology have taken the lead in the field of forensics. Counseling, again echoing history, is slow to start but fast in catching up. The value of scientific forensic to criminal investigations made the field increasingly crucial for evidence conclusions and criminal convictions. And from the valuation of scientific forensics arose the belief that an intersection between psychology and the justice system could also be beneficial to the compiling of evidence and to understanding the criminal mind. Forensic psychology's roots involve understanding criminal law and interpreting evidence to help judges, attorneys, and other legal professionals comprehend otherwise misunderstood or nonunderstandable information. The forensic psychologist's work involves testifying in court to reformulate psychological findings in the legal language of the court, making evidence of a psychological nature understandable and useful to court personnel.

The work of a forensic psychiatrist or psychologist runs more along the lines of assessing mental competency for an insanity plea, evaluating for malingering and competency, predicting future rehabilitation or recidivism, assessing personal injury, interpreting standardized assessment instruments, and conducting personality assessment. More recently, such work has also included evaluating child custody cases. It is the job of the forensic psychiatrist or psychologist to reword psychological data using legal terminology to help the court better understand the accused. For example, if the forensic psychologist is appointed by the court to assess the defendant's mind at the time of the crime, then the forensic psychologist is, in legal terms, being asked to assess whether the defendant, if he or she is found guilty, should be held criminally responsible for the crime owing to his or her degree of sanity at the time. In other words, the forensic psychologist is being asked by the court to act on obtained psychological data using his or her professional expertise to make a judgment. This judgment will help the court find a defendant competent to stand trial (or otherwise) and inform a verdict regarding whether a defendant who has been found guilty is criminally sane and was responsible for the crime.

Forensic psychologists and psychiatrists also provide sentencing recommendations to the court. They can give treatment recommendations, explain mitigating factors, assess future risk, and predict positive or negative outcomes, in addition to providing other information requested by the judge. Additionally, outside the courtroom, forensic psychologists facilitate training opportunities for attorneys and law enforcement. This training often gives attorneys and law enforcement officers guidelines to help them better judge defendants' degree of sanity as well as their motivation. Such training can also include sessions explaining how to converse and question in such ways as to acquire more accurate information. Additionally, forensic psychologists or psychiatrists often help assess prospective recruits into police academies and provide services to employed law enforcement personnel. They may also supply criminal profiles, help with jury selection, and provide other appropriate information assisting lawyers, judges, and law enforcement officers.

Thus, the scope of forensics has expanded from determining which sickle was used to kill the victim to using psychological data to make recommendations to the court regarding criminal responsibility. And forensic psychiatrists and psychologists have opened up yet another area of forensics to the expertise of their specific professions, this time dealing with the family law court to provide insight into custody evaluation, mediation, guardianship, adoption, and case management.

FORENSICS AND THE PROFESSIONAL COUNSELOR

Professional counselors have realized that they, too, have training and abilities allowing them to make psychological data understandable from legal and lay standpoints. They can also assess for mental competency and evaluate for malingering and competency to stand trial. Professional counselors can interpret standardized assessment instruments and make personality assessments. They can predict future recidivism and provide sentencing recommendations. Certainly they can provide child custody evaluations. Additionally, professional counselors can supply the training and evaluations needed by law enforcement officers and the court. They can help lawyers, judges, law enforcement officers, jurors, and all others involved in such cases understand psychological jargon from both legal and everyday perspectives. And they can teach other professionals how to learn and use better communications skills to acquire information useful for their specific needs.

TRAINING REQUIREMENTS

But psychiatrists, psychologists, clinical social workers, and professional counselors need additional training to provide all these forensic services. Ethically, none of these professions allows practice beyond a practitioner's established scope of competency. Just because you are a licensed psychiatrist, psychologist, clinical social worker, or counselor does not mean you can start practicing in forensics without further training, supervision, and experience. But once having acquired such additional training under appropriate supervision, professional counselors, because of their prior training and the philosophical foundations of the counseling profession, may be more particularly useful to courts than even other mental health professions are able to be—though surely practitioners of other mental health professions might disagree. However, professionals of every mental health profession agree on the importance of increasing training opportunities for their licensed providers. For these licensed professionals to begin providing forensic services to the courts, appropriate educational opportunities must arise at the grassroots level.

This text is one educational opportunity in a rather narrow area of forensics. The history of forensics is interesting, but the real work begins when a licensed professional starts the journey to actually providing service to a court. This book is narrow in its scope, focusing primarily on the forensic area of child custody evaluations; other texts spotlight mental competency, profiling, personality assessments, and still more services often provided by mental health professionals to the courts. This volume will take you on a journey toward becoming a custody evaluator. It will discuss the basics of the evaluation process; the things mental health professionals should focus on; methods to differentiate between reality and fantasy in this new world; and ways to provide recommendations that are meaningful and helpful to courts, parents, and children. This book is intended primarily for licensed professional counselors (LPCs; referred to as "counselors" hereafter) but can easily be understood and applied by practitioners in any of the other mental health professions.

So welcome to the interesting and challenging world of working in the family law system. Providing custody evaluations is challenging but can also be interesting, sometimes even entertaining. It is good work—different from therapy, but often just as rewarding. Let's get started!

2

Definitions of Legal Terms and Job Descriptions

Generally, all U.S. states share the same three-tiered court structure: The highest court in the state is the *state supreme court*. This court oversees the lower courts. The second tier is the *district courts*. The third tier is the *magistrate courts*, in some states called *county courts* or *general jurisdiction trial courts*. Magistrate courts deal with a wide variety of cases, such as traffic violations and misdemeanor violations. They also are responsible for decisions in cases concerning domestic relations, including divorce, alimony, child support, and child custody. When magistrate courts are dealing with family matters, they are often referred to as *family courts* or *family law courts*. Evaluators, mediators, and case managers generally work for magistrate courts.

Because court systems can vary, it is important that each forensic professional understand the court system in the state in which he or she practices. But equally important is understanding the language of the court. The legal system relies heavily on jargon, but in this chapter we will discuss only those terms and phrases most commonly used in family law. If you run across a term not explained here, don't assume that you know its meaning—look it up. Remember that different jurisdictions in different states can use different terms than those presented here. Always familiarize yourself with local terminology. Additionally, consider purchasing a dictionary of legal terms or finding one online.

COMMON LEGAL TERMS USED IN FAMILY COURT

AFCC: The Association of Family and Conciliation Courts, a professional organization dedicated to the resolution of family disputes.

Affidavit: A written statement made under oath by a party or witness. It is one way of presenting relevant facts to the court.

AKA: "Also known as," used to list aliases, previous names, or alternate spellings of a person's name.

Answer: A court document in which the defendant responds to the plaintiff's complaint.

Appeal: A procedure whereby a person challenges a decision made by a lower court about his or her case.

Applicant: The person who first comes to the court asking for a decision, also called the *plaintiff*, *petitioner*, or *complainant*.

Best interest of the child: The standard a judge uses when deciding custody and visitation issues.

Case: A lawsuit or action in a court.

Case assessment conference: The first court event for both parties to a case that is in progress in family court. This conference—attended by each party, each party's legal representation, and the judge—allows both sides to identify issues in dispute and future procedural steps, to appoint outside forensic professionals such as a custody evaluator or a mediator, and sometimes even to agree on a resolution to the case. The trial date can also be set at this conference. This conference provides both sides the opportunity to lay out their concerns and complaints before the judge so that everyone is on the same page. Not all jurisdictions hold case assessment conferences.

Case manager: A person, usually assigned by the court, who monitors and resolves parental disputes arising after an order has been entered by the court. Sometimes called a *special master*.

Case management directions: a set of directions given by the court to help the parties reach prompt and economical resolution, often written as a court order. For example, the court may direct both parties to see a custody evaluator and order that both pay half the evaluator's fee.

Child: a person younger than age 18 (in some jurisdictions, age 16 for custody cases).

Child custody and visitation recommendations report: The report generated by a child custody evaluator, which includes recommendations to the court regarding custody and visitation.

Child's representative: A lawyer appointed by the court to represent a child's interests in a case. This attorney, sometimes called a *separate representative* or *guardian ad litem*, attends all hearings and conducts the case in such a way as to promote the child's best interests. The guardian ad litem is served all court documents, is involved in all negotiations, and must approve any proposed arrangements.

Child support: The amount of money that one party must pay the other party each month to help financially support the child. The amount of child support is set by the court according to certain established guidelines.

Complainant: The person that first comes to the court asking for a decision, also called the *applicant, plaintiff,* or *petitioner*.

Court hearing: The date and time when the case is scheduled to come before the court.

Court order: Instructions by a court that both parties must carry out certain actions. A court order, sometimes called a *judgment* or *decree*, can be either final or interim.

Custody: An arrangement, determined by court order, indicating where a child will primarily live and how decisions about the child will be made.

Custody evaluator: A licensed professional, usually court-appointed, who provides recommendations about custody and visitation to the court with the child's best interest in mind. The evaluator is generally agreed upon by both parties.

Decision: Another term for the judgment of the court.

Defendant: The party who did not instigate the legal proceeding but who rather is defending his or her position against the claim filed by the plaintiff. Sometimes called the *respondent*.

Deposition: Testimony taken under oath, given outside the courtroom. A verbatim account (transcript) is made of the testimony.

Discovery: A process that requires either party to disclose to the other party all documents and witnesses relating to the case, including any written reports produced by evaluators or expert witnesses, so that they may be presented as evidence during the trial.

Divorce: The legal dissolution of a marriage.

Divorce order: An order made by the court that dissolves a marriage.

Divorce petition: An application to the court for divorce. This application also includes the plaintiff's requests for property division and for child custody and visitation arrangements.

Domestic violence: Conduct (either actual or threatened) by one person in a family towards another person in the family or that person's property, if the conduct causes reasonable fear for well-being. Also called *family violence*.

Evaluator: A professional person who is ordered by the court to conduct a child custody evaluation. Usually this person is agreed upon by both parties. Sometimes called a *custody evaluator*.

Evidence: Testimony, documents, or objects presented to the court in support of a point.

Ex parte hearing: A hearing for which one party is not present and of which that party has not been given notice before the court. This type of hearing is generally used only in emergencies.

Ex parte order: Evaluators work under a No Ex Parte Order: The evaluator must include both parties (generally both attorneys) in any discussions about the case.

Expert witness: A professional person hired by one of the parties to evaluate an aspect of a case. The expert witness usually does not work under a court order to conduct the evaluation. The cost of the evaluation is paid by the hiring party.

Family law courts: Magistrate courts dealing with family issues such as divorce, child custody, termination of parental rights, adoption, and guardianship.

Family violence: Conduct (either actual or threatened) by one person in a family toward another person in the family or that person's property, if the conduct causes reasonable fear for well-being. Also called *domestic violence*.

Final order: The order made by the court to conclude the case.

Guardian ad litem: An attorney chosen by the court to represent the child or children's interest in a family law case. Also called a *child's representative*.

In chambers: Discussion between the parties in the judge's office rather than in open court. Any decisions made in chambers must be put on the record in court.

Interim order: A temporary order.

Joint custody: A type of custody wherein both parents are responsible for protecting and caring for a child.

Judge: The person who makes the final decisions about the case and who issues a final order resolving and ending the case. Some states use a magistrate, a person who is not a judge but who is authorized to hear and decide certain types of cases. For example, family support magistrates hear some child support cases.

Legal custody: A relationship between a guardian and a child that is created by a court order giving a person legal responsibility for protecting and caring for the child.

Mediation: A dispute resolution process wherein an impartial trained third party helps the parties voluntarily reach a mutually acceptable resolution. In some jurisdictions, the mediation process is confidential and not available to the court.

Mediator: A professionally trained and impartial third party who attempts to help the parties reach a mutually agreed-upon resolution to their case.

Modification: An action requested by the plaintiff, the effect of which is to change the existing parenting plan. The modification request can include changes to the custody of the children, to the visitation schedule, to child support payments, or to any other aspect of the existing parenting plan.

NKA: "Now known as," used in reference to a person once known by one name but who is now using another name, an alias, or another spelling of his or her name.

No contact order: A court order prohibiting contact by one person with another person.

Order: A court document compelling a person to respond or to otherwise behave in a certain manner.

Order of evaluation: A court order appointing an evaluator to perform a parenting time evaluation, also called a *custody evaluation*.

Parental responsibility: The responsibility of both parents to make reasonable decisions regarding the care, welfare, and development of their child or children. These responsibilities may vary between the parents, either per agreement or per court order.

Parenting education program: A mandatory program or class for people involved in a divorce proceeding involving a child. This program attempts to teach parents how to handle the issues of divorce with the child and how to coparent the child in the future.

Parenting plan: A written agreement between both parties setting out the parenting arrangements for their children. Parenting plans can include custody, visitation schedules, child support, travel responsibilities, and exchange places and times, as well as any other responsibilities of the parents. The court must agree with the parenting plan and include it in a final order.

Parenting time evaluation: An investigation and analysis of the best interests of a child conducted by a licensed profession expert. The purpose of the evaluation is to provide recommendations that will help the court make decisions about custody and visitation orders.

Parties: Both the plaintiff and the defendant, and possibly other people whom the court allows to be involved in the case.

Petitioner: The person that first comes to the court asking for a decision, also called the *applicant, complainant,* or *plaintiff.*

Plaintiff: The party who instigates the legal proceedings, sometimes called the *complainant, applicant,* or *petitioner.*

Pretrial conference: A time for the parties and the judge to meet to discuss the case. Agreements are entered into the record. Any issues of dispute are also discussed. If an agreement is not reached at this time, then a trial date can be set for the case. Sometimes called a *preassessment conference.*

Primary physical custody: A custody arrangement created by a court order that provides for a child to spend more overnights with one parent than with the other during the course of the year.

Pro se: A party representing himself or herself in court without the aid of another party who is an attorney.

Protective order: A court order issued by a judge to protect a family or household member. This is sometimes called a *no contact order.*

Rules: The set of regulations and directions that outline the court's guidelines and procedures. These rules maintain similarity between different magistrate districts and different judges.

Second opinion evaluator: A professional person who conducts a second evaluation at the request of one of the parties. The second opinion evaluator is often working under a court order. The party requesting the second opinion is responsible for the costs incurred in obtaining the second opinion.

Service: The legal term for the giving or delivering of court documents to another person in an effort to make sure the person receives them. This is represented by the famous "You have been served" line from movies and television programs.

Shared custody: A court order providing virtually the same number of overnights to both parents. This is sometimes called *split custody*.

Sole custody: A court order providing for one parent to have the responsibility for protecting and caring for a child.

Special master: A person who is responsible for resolving conflicts between the parents subsequent to a court order of custody and visitation, usually court-appointed and agreed upon by both parties. Sometimes called a *case manager* or a *court-appointed case manager*.

Split custody: An order of the court providing for virtually equal overnights for both parents with a child. This is also called *shared custody*.

Subpoena: A document issued by the court requiring a person to appear in court at a certain date and time and possibly with documents specific in the subpoena. Ignoring a subpoena can result in fines or imprisonment.

Temporary custody/visitation: A court order placing a child in a short-term legal custodial arrangement. This order can also include a short-term visitation schedule for the child.

Testimony: Statements made by a witness under oath. The testimony becomes part of the official court record.

Transcript: The record of the spoken evidence presented in a court case. All court hearings are recorded. Transcripts are available upon request by either party. The requesting party is responsible for any costs associated with obtaining a transcript. Depositions are also recorded verbatim and are available as transcripts.

Trial: The final hearing before a judge. This is the opportunity for both parties to present their cases to the judge. The trial involves examination and cross-examination of witnesses, presentation of evidence (e.g., a child custody evaluator's written report), and final arguments. At the end of the trial, the judge issues a decision and finalizes orders concluding the case.

Visitation: The amount of time a parent may spend with his or her child, sometimes called *parenting time* or *access*.

Witness: A person who testifies in court about what he or she saw, heard, observed, or did.

EXPANDED DEFINITIONS OF CUSTODY EVALUATOR, CASE MANAGER, AND MEDIATOR

Some of these terms need further explanation and description. Remember: An evaluator is not an attorney and thus is not expected to be familiar with all legal jargon. However, the evaluator must understand the legal terms used in family law cases. If you don't know what something means, look it up. Don't hesitate to use a legal dictionary, and don't assume that you understand unless you know that you do. To help you with that, let's expand on the roles of custody evaluator, case manager, and mediator.

CUSTODY EVALUATOR

The custody evaluator is a licensed professional person usually appointed by the court to help the court better understand the issues, both apparent and underlying, surrounding a family going through divorce. Furthermore, his or her job is to give the court recommendations furthering the best interest of the child regarding custody and visitation. A custody evaluator is the child's voice in court. Most family courts do not require, or even allow, children to testify in open court. Decisions about which parent the child will live with most of the time and what visitation schedule is ideal for the child are best left to the parents and other adults.

Depending on the state, a custody evaluator generally is a licensed physician who has board certification in psychiatry, a licensed psychologist, a licensed clinical social worker or licensed social worker in private practice, a licensed clinical professional counselor, or a licensed marriage and family therapist. Regardless of terminology, the custody evaluator is licensed at the highest tier of his or her profession. Additionally, the licensed person must have completed a specified number of evaluations under the supervision of a qualified evaluator.

There are some exceptions to the licensing rule. A nonlicensed person may be selected by the court to conduct an evaluation supervised by a qualified person. For example, in some jurisdictions, a family court services staff member provides evaluations but must be supervised by a qualified and licensed person. Additionally, the court may appoint, or the parties may request, the appointment of a person who does not meet the licensing requirements. This person generally must have a license in some area relevant to families and children and must have conducted a certain number of evaluations prior to his or her appointment. Rules differ by state, so discover what the qualifications are in your state and jurisdiction. An evaluator's qualifications provide the court with an assurance that the evaluator's professional expertise will help the court make a reasoned and thoughtful judgment upholding the best interest of the child.

Four Components: Education, Therapeutic Expertise, Supervision, Practice

Education

There are four main components to an effective evaluator, mediator, or case manager: education, therapeutic expertise, supervision, and practice. An evaluator must have the educational foundation for understanding the dynamics of a family, including a divorcing family. In addition, an evaluator must be well read in the area of divorce and its short- and long-term effects on parents and children.

Furthermore, the people who come to the evaluator's office are those who cannot resolve the issues that face them. People who have decided on divorce do not need a marriage therapist for an evaluator. They need someone to understand their side of the issues, to understand the best interest of the child involved in the case, and to make recommendations to the court protecting the best interest of the child. In other words, it is the evaluator's job to protect the child's best interests while dealing with the realities of the case. It is not the evaluator's job to advise the parents on their decision or to try to reunite the parents.

Some of the cases an evaluator deals with are not divorce but are rather modifications to custody, to the visitation schedule, or to guardianship, or they seek to establish a visitation schedule between unmarried parents. Such issues are better dealt with by an evaluator whose educational background helps him or her understand the adults' and children's concerns.

Therapeutic Expertise

The second component of an evaluator is his or her therapeutic expertise. Generally, successful evaluators are also successful in a therapeutic practice. To be an effective evaluator, the therapeutic skills of empathy, unconditional positive regard, understanding, listening, reflection, and emotional awareness are critical. Evaluation is certainly not therapy, but the skills necessary to being a successful counselor are also necessary to becoming a successful evaluator. The evaluator understands emotions, whether underlying or exposed. He or she also can discern between genuine emotional expression and an attempt to just say "the right thing." Just as a good counselor in therapy recognizes incongruencies, so does a good evaluator.

Reflection, confrontation, and active listening are essential tools in the evaluation process. Even though the evaluation process is not a therapy session, the skills a counselor uses in a counseling session are those he or she also uses in an evaluation session. The evaluator must be able to reflect feelings, actively listen, and confront as necessary. The evaluation process is not just a series of questions; it is a time for the parent or child to tell his or her story and discuss the issues and emotions surrounding the divorce. It is a time for the evaluator to clarify emotions, understand underlying motives, clarify parenting skills (or lack thereof), and paint himself or herself a picture of the case to understand how to best meet the needs of the child.

Supervision

The supervision process may be the primary vehicle by which a novice becomes a successful evaluator, mediator, or case manager. A new evaluator must find a seasoned evaluator to be his or her mentor and supervisor. The supervision this mentor provides will give the rookie the experience, knowledge, and confidence to be successful.

The supervisor should be a person who meets the qualifications of an evaluator and who has been doing evaluations for an extended period of time. He or she should be a person who has successfully helped courts make orders best meeting the needs of children in custody cases and should also have built a reputation of fairness and objectivity within the court system, as well as a reputation for excellence among family law attorneys, who request evaluators, recommend evaluators to other attorneys, and promote the role of the evaluator. Without the trust of the family law attorneys, an evaluator will get little work. Attorneys must view an evaluator as fair and unbiased to either side of a family law case. They must believe that the evaluator has the expertise, including the education and the practice, required to make recommendations to the court that are fair, reasonable, and based on professional opinions. Although any family law attorney wants the evaluator to weigh in on the side of his or her client, he or she wants even more to know that the evaluator has entered into the case without biases and prejudices toward either side, that the evaluator will treat each case on its own merits and make recommendations to the court that are focused on the child's best interests. The attorneys expect the evaluator to be consistent and compelling in court.

Finding the right supervisor may not be easy, but it is essential for earning the respect of the court and of family law attorneys. Therefore, ask family law attorneys who they recommend for evaluations, and ask people who have been through the evaluation process who their evaluator was and what they thought of him or her. If you have the opportunity, ask a family court judge which evaluators he or she likes to have testify in his or her courtroom. Ask whose recommendations for custody and visitation make the most sense and are most helpful to the judge. These evaluators make the best supervisors.

Supervision: Phase 1 The supervision process needs to include every aspect of the case from inception to resolution. For the novice evaluator, the first step is observing the seasoned evaluator in action. Sit in on each session, reading the documentation that comes with the case. Listen to the conversations the evaluator has with collateral contacts. Talk to the evaluator about his or her thoughts about the case throughout. Understand why the evaluator makes the recommendations he or she does about custody and visitation. Be involved when the evaluator consults with the attorneys before appearing in court. Finally, observe the evaluator when he or she testifies in court. In other words: Be the supervisor's shadow. Ask questions, give ideas, listen and observe.

Supervision: Phase 2 In the second phase of supervision, the novice evaluator will conduct an evaluation under the close supervision of the seasoned evaluator. Allow the supervisor into sessions and consultations and let him or her watch you writing your recommendations. Consult with the supervisor every step along the way. Ask for help, guidance, and supervision. With each successive case, your supervisor can be less involved; however, don't just abandon the supervision process. At minimum, take at least five supervised cases before taking cases alone. Remember: Even seasoned evaluators need to consult with other professionals occasionally about a case. The more cases an evaluator handles, the more confidence he or she has in the process and in his or her own recommendations.

And thus the fourth component is practice. Practice makes a counselor good and makes a good counselor better. Practice is also what makes a good evaluator. Remember when you first learned the counseling skills—how awkward they sometimes felt. Reflect on the first client you counseled and how inept you felt. Now remember how, many clients and hours of practice later, you feel like a "real" counselor. Clients bring a wide variety of issues to the table, but you can handle what they present. Practice made that possible. And so is it with custody evaluations.

Practice

Practice allows the evaluator to refine the process that works best for himself or herself. He or she can identify the key issues in any case to better understand the parents' perspectives. With practice, the evaluator can understand the issues the children bring to the case. Practice increases the efficiency of the evaluator's use of time and energy, and it also brings the confidence that an evaluator needs if he or she is to be maximally effective.

Practice also strengthens the evaluator's reputation with the judges and the attorneys. A reputation for fairness, reliability, efficiency, and understanding the realities of each case brings more business to the evaluator's practice. All four components are important, but reputation allows the evaluator to flourish in forensic practice. Building a reputation takes educational background, therapeutic expertise, supervision, and practice; however, without a reputation for professionalism, the evaluator will simply not be asked to provide recommendations to the court regarding custody and visitation.

CASE MANAGER

A case manager is a professional person who generally meets the same qualifications of an evaluator but who may be an attorney. Nevertheless, a case manager must still have the expertise to understand child developmental issues, issues of emotional stress, issues associated with divorce, and parental motivations. The cases generally assigned to a case manager are those that have reached a certain level of chaos, revenge, and out-of-control parental behavior. In these cases, neither parent is willing to coparent, listen, negotiate, or even acknowledge that the other parent has any parenting ability at all. In such cases, which are constantly before the court, supervision is needed for the parents. Therefore, a case manager is assigned.

A case manager does not make recommendations to the court but rather acts on the court's behalf to reduce conflicts between the parents and to make decisions for the parents that are in the child's best interests. The case manager listens to both parents' complaints and makes a judgment about how to resolve the conflict. Generally, the case manager has the authority to make decisions about such issues as visitation schedules, exchange times and places, and how to remediate questionable parenting skills.

Being a case manager is not a job for an easily frustrated person or someone without an unending store of patience. The continuous chaos the parents have created over a lengthy period often borders on ridiculous. The case manager must listen, understand both sides of the issues, and make decisions the parents must abide by to reduce the conflict. And then the next conflict raises its ugly head—and then the next.

A case manager not only needs to have the skills of an evaluator, but also must be able to establish and maintain boundaries with the parents. He or she must also be able to manage the money paid to the case manager as a retainer, making it very clear how the parents can contact the case manager and how much money will be charged for each contact. He or she must also be able to make reasonable and timely decisions to resolve conflicts as quickly as possible. Last, a good case manager must have the ability to train the parents to make decisions between themselves and by themselves through coparenting.

MEDIATOR

A mediator is a professional person educated in the areas of an evaluator but who additionally has the skills and education to deal with the money and property issues of the divorcing family. A mediator is often an attorney and thus has the educational background to deal with issues of child support, debt, and asset division. A custody evaluator does not usually deal with money issues in any depth, whereas a mediator must help the parents agree on how to divide money and property. Occasionally, mediation deals strictly with custody and visitation or strictly with financial issues only. Nevertheless, a mediator needs the education and skills to create an atmosphere between parents that fosters negotiation and compromise with an eye to resolution.

A mediator has the skills necessary to maintain a businesslike atmosphere during the mediation. A mediation session is not the time for either parent to complain about the other. It is not the time to tell stories about the failure of the family. It is not the time for either parent to place blame on the other parent. Instead, the mediator keeps the parents on track to help them reach resolution on a variety of issues in a realistic, non-emotional, businesslike manner. This is not a job for the faint of heart: Each parent generally wants the other parent to pay for his or her offenses (whether real or imagined). The mediator must keep emotions out of the discussion, understand each parent's side, and discover what will most perfectly meet the child's best interests. Additionally, he or she must also understand the guidelines for child support, alimony, spousal support, debt payment, and asset division.

A skilled mediator helps the parents reach closure in the areas of custody, visitation, child support, debt payment, and asset division. Generally, the discussions held during mediation are confidential and cannot be reported to the court or even to the attorneys. The agreed-upon solutions are reported, but the discussions leading to those solutions are not. If mediation fails, it is reported to the court as a failure, but the reasons for failure nevertheless remain confidential.

However, there are similarities as well as differences in the training and expertise of evaluators, case managers, and mediators. One common thread between these professionals is that each belongs to and supports professional organizations that not only promote a specific profession but also unify forensic experts. A general discussion of these organizations follows.

PROFESSIONAL ORGANIZATIONS OF FORENSIC EXPERTS

National and State Professional Organizations

Professional organizations define their associated profession. Without professional organizations, there is no profession. Therefore, it is responsible behavior for a professional person to be a member of his or her respective professional organization. For example, many forensic experts are members of the American Counseling Association and the American Psychological Association.

Being a member of your professional organization is only a first step. Attending conferences on both the state and national levels is the next. Professional conferences provide training in the field of forensics, allowing you to update your store of knowledge and expertise. The conferences also provide opportunities to interact with others across the country who are engaged in work with family courts. Talking to these people is a good way to build relationships with others who do the same work as you, possibly developing sources for future consultations at the same time. Last, being more involved in the professional organization by taking leadership positions and providing actual training sessions during the conference is another way to promote the work of forensic experts in the family courts.

Still another professional organization to which many forensic experts belong is the Association of Family and Conciliation Courts (AFCC), which focuses on the issues before family courts and those who work within the family court system. Although it is not as well known as the ACA or APA, it has significantly affected the family court system and the work of forensic experts.

Association of Family and Conciliation Courts

The Association of Family and Conciliation Courts (AFCC) is an interdisciplinary and international association promoting resolution of family conflict. Although the members are not all of a single profession, they all share a commitment to promoting education and collaboration in an effort to empower families, promote healthy children, and reduce conflicts in families. Over the past 50 years, the AFCC has generated major reforms and guidelines for family and divorce mediation, child custody evaluations, case management, and court-involved therapy and educational opportunities.

AFCC's journal, the *Family Court Review*, is one of the leading interdisciplinary family law journals. The *Family Court Review* publishes on topics such as domestic violence, child development and attachment, parental alienation, family courts, and mediation. This journal prints many articles helpful to both evolving and seasoned evaluators, mediators, and case managers. It is also a source of helpful information for counselors employed by the courts to provide educational opportunities to parents and children, as well as counseling services.

Since its inception in California in 1963, the AFCC has grown to international status and now includes a wide variety of professionals, ranging from judges and lawyers to counselors, psychologists, court administrators, and financial planners as members. The AFCC grew from a few California judges to a significant group providing services and guidelines for court-connected services in courts in states including Hawaii, Idaho, Ohio, Oregon, Michigan, Arizona, and Montana, as well as in several Canadian provinces. Other states are actively investigating the family courts in these states, and many are currently in the process of establishing—or have already established—similar guidelines and procedures.

The AFCC was responsible for establishing a pilot program in the early 1970s for mediating custody and visitation disputes. About that time, divorce education workshops for parents also began to be ordered in family courts. As the value of mediation and parent education became apparent, more family courts in more states began to change strategies and embrace the concepts originally promoted by the AFCC.

In the 1980s, court-connected reconciliation counseling was diminishing as joint custody, mediation, divorce education, coparenting, domestic violence, and stepparenting skills moved to the forefront in family courts. Mandatory mediation and joint custody were issues regularly considered in courts in many states. By the late 1980s, mandatory mediation of custody and visitation disputes was established in more than 33 states. Furthermore, mothers' economic struggles subsequent to divorce and groups advocating parental rights for fathers moved more jurisdictions to view mediation and evaluations as viable tools for settling divorce issues. Child developmental issues subsequent to the breakup of the family were also studied, including in scholarly articles. Family courts, seeing more divorce actions than before, needed a way to deal fairly with both parents while protecting the best interests of the child. Therefore, the AFCC began to develop guidelines for helping family courts deal with difficult cases of divorce.

High-conflict families, domestic violence, and the effects of divorce on children were catalysts for the AFCC's development of guidelines helping family courts assist parents in reaching resolution and helping family court judges produce orders improving and protecting the life of the child affected by the family conflict.

The agenda of the AFCC has changed over the years from reconciliation to divorce with dignity to mandated mediation to work with high-conflict and violent families. The AFCC continues to refine the guidelines used by many states and jurisdictions to reflect the changes in today's culture. Courts are now dealing not only with the traditional divorcing family but also with pro se litigants, same-sex partnerships, never-married parents, domestic abuse, case management, custody evaluations, relocation of parents, and alienated children. The challenges are many.

Myths and Truths About Working in Family Law Courts

It is important for an evaluator who works in family court to have a clear understanding of what is true and what is not when it comes to work in family law. Your job is to ignore common myths and instead discover the truth. But remember that even these truths are generalizations that may not hold true in all cases. Never forget that each case stands on its own merits and needs to be dealt with accordingly.

MYTH #1: IN THE LONG RUN, A CHILD IS NOT HARMED BY A DIVORCE

Truth #1: Years ago mental health professionals were trained that children, given the passage of time, suffered no lasting effects from divorce. People generally believed that children "snapped out" of any emotional or behavioral problems caused by a divorce. Such beliefs may have relieved the guilt that adults felt for divorcing, but they were untrue. Divorce changes a child's life forever.

True, some damage done to the child by a divorce may not be severe or debilitating. It may not hinder the child's ability to move forward positively in life. It may not provoke a chronic mental illness, but even so it never stops affecting the child. Every child suffers when his or her family is broken apart. Numerous studies, some longitudinal, now

25

verify that divorce detrimentally affects children. The effects of divorce last into adulthood for all children. Furthermore, how a child deals with the divorce and the damage that divorce causes is directly related to how the parents handle the divorce itself and how much conflict the child sees between the parents.

Parents want the evaluator to tell them that everything will be all right, both for them and for their children. They want to hear that the divorce, the fighting between the parents, the child's new life in two homes and as part of two families—that all this will turn out to be a good thing, not something that causes their child harm. A good evaluator, like a good counselor, never lies to his or her client. Things will be different, but not all things will be good—some may well be as bad as or worse than they were before the divorce. Children will carry the scars of the divorce as it affects them throughout their entire lives. The amount of damage the child suffers depends on both parents. Whether the wound heals into a thin scar or remains a gaping, festering wound depends on the people who caused the damage in the first place. The parents who chose to break apart the family also have the responsibility to decide how detrimental the breakup will be to their child.

Certainly there can be good reasons for dissolving a marriage. Remember that it isn't the evaluator's job to try to reunite the parents; rather, he or she tries to resolve conflict so that the child can be cared for by two parents who act reasonably and responsibly to coparent. The evaluator's job is to help the courts issue orders that are in the child's best interest and that mitigate the damage to the child that is inherent in a divorce.

MYTH #2: MOTHERS ARE USUALLY CONSIDERED THE PRIMARY CAREGIVERS OF THE CHILD AND ARE THEREFORE GENERALLY GRANTED PRIMARY CUSTODY

Truth #2: In the past this was true. Mothers were often automatically assumed to be the child's primary caregivers and were thus granted primary custody. Fathers were granted only visitation rights, often consisting of alternate weekend visitation. Mothers were viewed as the most important person in a child's life.

But over the years research has shown that although mothers are important in a child's life, fathers are equally important. The father's role is not dismissed in today's courts. Fathers are as important as mothers: Each child needs a father in his or her life if he or she is to grow positively and become emotionally well-adjusted. The role of the father must be consistent and continuous. Understandably, children are better off and grow up better adjusted emotionally and psychologically when both their parents play a primary role in their lives.

Thus, in today's family courts, mothers are not automatically granted primary custody. Rather, the court now weighs all the evidence and decides not only who is the primary caregiver, but also which parent can provide the most stability and consistency for the child and which parent is more likely to facilitate coparenting between the two parents. Today, fathers are as likely as mothers to be given primary custody. Shared custody arrangements are also used wherein both parents have approximately equal access to the child in their respective homes. The family court realizes that a man can care for a child just as well as a woman can. Men can do the laundry, cook, clean, and help with homework. Men are no longer viewed as incompetent bystanders when it comes to raising children, but rather as equally competent parents in the child-rearing process. Furthermore, courts recognize that what fathers offer their children is different from what mothers offer, and equally important to a child's development. Today's court orders reflect this improved understanding of the father–child bond.

In some cases, men appear to be treated differently from women, but these cases are becoming rarer. More and more orders coming out of family courts recognize the importance of the father, and you also must do the same. A fair and reasonable evaluator does not begin the evaluation with a bias toward or against either parent, but rather believes that both parents have something important to offer the child. In some instances, this assumption may prove to be untrue, but you must start the evaluation without prejudice against either parent and continue until you determine otherwise, if ever.

MYTH #3: BOTH PARENTS IN A CUSTODY BATTLE DESIRE WHAT IS BEST FOR THEIR CHILD

Truth #3: It is true that both parents *think* that what they want is best for their child. Unfortunately, this generally includes wanting limited or no access to the child by the other parent. Certainly there are cases in which one parent needs to have limited, supervised, or even no access to the child. But these cases are relatively rare.

Often what is really happening is that one or both parents are moti-
vated not by care for their child but rather by a desire to exact revenge
on the other parent. An evaluator must always be aware of a parent's
underlying need for revenge regardless of the parent's words. Many
times this need for revenge outweighs the parent's love for the child, so
it is important that the evaluator be cognizant of the parent's underlying motives.

Sometimes, however, revenge is not the motivating factor—money
is. Both parents may want what is best for the child, but also what is best
for their wallet. Child support is calculated on the number of overnights
a child has with the parent during the year. In some states, guidelines
for calculating child support are based on income and overnight per-
centage. Thus, some parents say they want what is best for the child but
actually want to host the majority of overnights in order to get more or
pay less child support. An evaluator does not deal with child support
figures, but the evaluator does recommend a visitation schedule that is
best for the child—without considering whether it is best for a parent's
bank account.

MYTH #4: CHILDREN OF A CERTAIN AGE (GENERALLY AGE 12) CAN DECIDE WHERE THEY WANT TO LIVE AND HOW OFTEN THEY VISIT THE OTHER PARENT

Truth #4: Many people believe that when a child reaches a certain age—
generally age 12–14—he or she can then decide his or her own custody
and visitation schedule. This is untrue. A child may decide where he
or she lives and who he or she visits at age 18 (in some jurisdictions,
age 16). It is up to the evaluator to know what the rules are in his or
her jurisdiction. However, no child has the right or the responsibility
to decide a custody and visitation schedule before reaching adulthood.

Of course the child has a voice in the process, but that voice is not
the final word. An evaluator listens to the child and hears what he or she
has to say about the breakup of his or her family. The evaluator hears
the child's feelings and is the child's voice in court. However, that does
not mean the evaluator has to agree with everything the child thinks
will work best for himself or herself. It does not mean that the evaluator
directly asks the child what parent he or she wants to live with or what
schedule he or she wishes for visitations with the other parent. When

a child tells the evaluator what schedule he or she thinks would work best, the evaluator will ask why the child thinks his or her suggested schedule is best. But even this does not mean the evaluator will go along with what the child says.

It is not good parenting for a parent to allow the child to make decisions that are not his or hers to make. Often evaluators will hear from a certain parent that the child wants to live with him or her or wants to visit the other parent on a certain schedule. The evaluator needs to explore how this conversation started: what the child said, what the parent said, and how the parent handled the situation. It is telling when a parent does not understand that a child is not in a position to make these kinds of decisions but instead abdicates his or her own responsibilities to the child.

There certainly are cases when the child is thinking more clearly than his or her parents; in such a case, the child may well understand how to facilitate his or her own best interests. But generally the child's decisions focus on keeping one parent happy and trying to squelch the conflict between the parents. The evaluator needs to listen carefully to the child while remembering that these difficult decisions are not the child's responsibility.

MYTH #5: STEPPARENTS HAVE A SAY IN MATTERS OF CUSTODY AND VISITATION SCHEDULE

Truth #5: Stepparents have no legal rights when it comes to their stepchildren. For example, they have no rights of access to legal records, school records, or medical records. They have no right to influence the stepchild's custody and visitation schedule. That said, stepparents are usually highly involved in their stepchildren's lives.

Stepparents certainly help raise their stepchildren. A good stepparent establishes appropriate boundaries on his or her role as it involves the stepchild, the custodial parent, and the other parent. Many custody battles and modifications take place because the stepparent is not happy with the current situation. He or she may feel it necessary to defend his or her significant other or feel responsible to facilitate communication between the parents—or even handle all communication with the other parent. The stepparent may feel as if the stepchild is his or her child and view the other parent as a bother that needs to be eliminated from the child's life. The stepparent may be angry that child support money is being paid to another person instead of being spent on his or her own family. Regardless of how the stepparent feels, it is not his or her place to hold sway over matters of custody and visitation.

In any evaluation, the stepparent or the person acting like a stepparent (e.g., when a parent and another are living together unmarried) is involved in the evaluation process. Because he or she is now a part of the child's life in the new family, the evaluator has to understand the stepparent's parenting skills as well as his or her stability and ability to establish appropriate boundaries. Often the stepparent accompanies the parent to the interview. This allows the evaluator to see firsthand how involved, overbearing, supportive, or manipulating the stepparent can be. Holding a joint interview allows the evaluator to establish who primarily cares for the child—the parent or the stepparent. It allows the evaluator to determine whether the stepparent is taking over the responsibilities of the parent regarding communication, scheduling, and family values. The evaluator can also determine how involved the stepparent is in the conflict between the two parents and how much the stepparent "stirs the pot."

A stepparent should be supportive of the parent and should also be understanding of the other parent's concerns. He or she should understand that he or she is not the parent of the stepchild, but rather another adult who adds depth and difference to the child's life. A functional stepparent does not do the communicating between the parents but rather facilitates communication. He or she does not take over the parent's responsibilities and duties, but rather enhances the parent's abilities. He or she does not speak poorly about the other parent and instead is supportive of the child's feelings toward both the child's parents. A stepparent does not put his or her biological children before the stepchild, but rather makes every effort to treat all the children in the family fairly and respectfully.

A wise parent makes every effort to get along with the stepparent and to encourage the child to have a functional relationship with the stepparent. It is good when a child likes his or her stepparent; such a relationship is not a threat to a parent and his or her relationship with the child. Rather, because the child is at the stepparent's home and is being taken care of by the stepparent, a thoughtful parent sees this as good for his or her child and good for continued coparenting with the other parent. Children, like adults, have the capacity to like and love many people. A stepparent as an ally is better for coparenting and certainly better for the child than is a stepparent as an enemy.

MYTH #6: PUTTING TWO DIFFERENT FAMILIES TOGETHER AS ONE IS RELATIVELY EASY

Truth #6: Parents who divorce and remarry (or live together) want this to be true. They don't want any trials, tribulations, or conflict in the new family. But putting two different families together is as difficult as getting ultraconservatives and ultraliberals into the same political bed. It doesn't happen without a lot of work, time, patience, and effort—and sometimes it doesn't work even after that. Just because two adults want to be together and care for each other does not mean that the children in their two families will care for their new stepsiblings' or stepparent's invasion of their family.

Blending two families can cause as much emotional distress to a child as the original divorce did. The parent is now asking the child not only to deal with the breakup of the original family and to learn the new rules, regulations, and schedules of his or her parents' new homes while dealing with the emotional upheavals of the parents, but also to abide by another set of rules, regulations, and schedules in a new home with a stepparent who takes the child's parent away from the child—and to live with other children who are also trying to learn the new family format and share their own parent with this new stepparent. The child no longer has his or her parent and his or her own space, but now must share with other children he or she may not even like. That's a lot to ask of a child without expecting some collateral damage.

Often an evaluator hears from a parent that the blended family is working wonderfully. The parent reports that all the children love each other and get along famously. There were virtually no problems putting the two families together, says the parent: Everyone is happy and loving. A savvy evaluator knows that such an occurrence is vanishingly rare. Families almost never come together without problems, trials, and conflict.

It speaks volumes to an evaluator how quickly parents move on to create another family regardless of how difficult doing so is for their child. Rebound relationships generally turn out poorly. Blended families from these relationships often do not work out. It is not particularly good parenting to insist that a child raw from a divorce gracefully mix with another family. It takes an enormous amount of patience and coparenting to make this a successful transition for the child. The evaluator has to wonder whether the parent is looking more toward his or her own happiness rather than the positive development of his or her child.

MYTH #7: ONE PARENT HOLDS THE TRUTH TO WHAT HAPPENED IN A DIVORCING FAMILY

Truth #7: Both parents have a story to tell about what happened in the family, what is currently happening, and what will work best for their child. Both parents have different perspectives on what caused the divorce and on the resulting conflict between the parents. Neither parent is totally right nor totally wrong. Each parent's perspective on what has happened and what continues to happen is just that: a perspective.

It is the evaluator's job to listen with a critical ear, hearing not just the words of the parent's story but also the underlying emotions and motivations. The parent should also provide some validation of his or her claims. For example, during the interview, a parent might tell the evaluator that the other parent has an alcohol problem, claiming that he or she drinks to excess regularly and has used illegal drugs in the past, insisting that the other parent have limited access to the child because of the parent's alcoholism. The evaluator might ask whether the other parent has been arrested for drunkenness, including for driving while intoxicated, or has been arrested for drug use and whether the other parent behaves dangerously under the effects of alcohol or drugs. If not, then does the other parent really have an alcohol problem? Or is this parent trying to influence the visitation schedule? The evaluator should check with other people who can verify the parent's claims—without more than the word of one parent, the parent's concern might not suffice to affect the outcome of the case even if there really is a problem.

Remember: This case wouldn't exist if both parents agreed. There is conflict because each parent has a different opinion about what happened, what is happening, and what is best for the child. The parents' stories are far apart and in some aspects removed from reality. Memories are not always accurate. Desires and strong emotions blur the lines between reality and belief. It need not be that the parent is lying to the evaluator; rather, his or her memories may have been tainted by time, emotional pain, need for revenge, hurt, anger, or any other of a multitude of emotions. The evaluator should hear the parent's words but also hear the parent's emotions.

Neither parent is entirely right, nor entirely wrong. After hearing one parent the novice evaluator can find it easy to take that parent's story as gospel and to subsequently make mental recommendations for custody and visitation before hearing the other parent's version of what happened. Such preconceptions are always a mistake. No matter how dreadful a person one parent made the other parent out to be, when the evaluator hears the other parent speak, he or she is now hearing the other side of the story. The evaluator's job is to gather information from everyone before arriving at recommendations that seek the child's best interests. It is the evaluator's job to paint a picture of these parents, this child, this conflict, and this case by gathering all the facts of the case—and to not do so until then. Doing so requires hearing all sides of the story, necessarily from all its participants. Until the picture is complete, the evaluator cannot make helpful recommendations to the court, allowing the judge to issue orders that best serve the child.

MYTH #8: EVALUATORS ARE ALWAYS RIGHT, AND THEIR RECOMMENDATIONS ARE ALWAYS FOLLOWED BY THE COURT

Truth #8: If only evaluators' recommendations *were* always correct. If only evaluators always wrote the best possible recommendations for the child. That's the goal. Evaluators are trained to hear what lies behind the spoken words of the parents and child. They are trained to follow ethical guidelines, the guidelines of the AFCC, and the rules of the courts. But evaluators are still people, and sometimes they make mistakes. Their recommendations might be missing something or may be poorly communicated and thus misunderstood. Or an evaluator may simply get caught up in the case.

Every evaluator wants to do the best work possible, to speak for the child whose voice has been lost. Every evaluator wants to speak on the parents' behalf to resolve conflict, encouraging healthy growth for the child. Every evaluator wants to help the court write the order that best meets the needs of the child and that best helps the parents resolve their differences. Every evaluator wants to help parents become effective coparents who can raise a child to be a functioning member of society. So when an evaluator writes recommendations, he or she bases them on his or her professional opinion of the evidence, including the parents' parenting abilities and the child's developmental needs. A solid and communicable rationale for a recommendation means that the evaluator did his or her job, speaking for the child. Without such a rationale, the court cannot issue an order in the child's best interest. In this case, the evaluator will have left himself or herself open to a potentially nerve-wracking cross-examination.

Attorneys look forward to questioning an evaluator in court. If the evaluator's recommendations are lacking or otherwise of insufficient quality, this will not be a pleasant experience for the evaluator, although it may be a very pleasant experience for the attorney. Family law attorneys have a sense for what makes a good recommendation, and it is their job to find the weak link in your report. A good family law attorney will represent his or her client's position in court regardless of an evaluator's recommendations. It is not the evaluator's job to make doing this any easier for the attorney. Base your recommendations on solid reasoning, and be prepared to give a clear and convincing rationale. And if you are wrong, then admit it. Remember: Writing a recommendation that carries the potential for harm to the child or his or her family is the antithesis of your work. You must be thoughtful in your recommendations, and you must base them on a good understanding of the issues in the case at hand.

MYTH #9: ALL FAMILY LAW CASES ARE GENERALLY EQUIVALENT

Truth #9: Nothing could be farther from the truth. No case is equivalent to another. Similarities may exist among cases, but they are just that: similarities.

Evaluators follow a certain protocol for interviewing: who to interview, who to get in touch with as collateral contacts, how to write a recommendation. This structure gives the evaluator a place to start, then allows him or her to start filling in the blanks, getting answers that can direct his or her recommendations to the court. An evaluation protocol is much like a house's foundation, which dictates the size and shape of the building but does not determine how many rooms will be built, nor their color or furnishings. Similarly, the evaluation protocol structures the interviews without stifling the process. Because all interviews are focused by the evaluation protocol, they may see similar questions asked by the evaluator, but the information gleaned will be unique to the case at hand. It is the evaluator's training that provides him or her with the flexibility and understanding to allow each case to stand on its own merits.

A seasoned evaluator knows that he or she has never heard it all when it comes to forensics in the family law arena. And so the evaluator knows that structure in the evaluation is all well and good—but flexibility is the key to understanding human behavior, emotion, and motivations, as well as the road to both the parents and the child functioning in positive, growth-producing ways. No two cases are identical. Nor any two humans. Nor any two families. Nor any two children, nor judges, nor attorneys—nor evaluators. But all evaluators are trained professionally to work with children and families and are trained in forensics to make recommendations that facilitate the child's best interests. How they achieve this may be different, but the result is similar for all evaluators.

MYTH #10: ALL FAMILY COURTS AND ALL JURISDICTIONS USE CUSTODY EVALUATORS

Truth #10: More and more jurisdictions are relying on the services of custody evaluators. However, depending on where you live and practice, this may not be the case. It may be up to you to educate local judges, attorneys, and parents about the benefits of using custody evaluation to resolve disputes.

Some courts still try to resolve family conflicts using the criminal model of trial, evidence, and testimony—when dealing not only with adults, but also with the child. These courts put the child in the witness stand to testify and be cross-examined by attorneys in front of the child's parents. As outdated and detrimental as this sounds, it still happens. However, no child should be forced to face the two people that he or she loves most and make one the "bad guy" and one the "good guy." No child should have to choose between his or her parents. And no child should be forced to decide his or her own fate by making adult decisions.

If you live in a jurisdiction that does not rely on custody evaluators, it is your job to introduce the value of this service to the courts. You should present the benefits to attorneys at continuing education sessions and ask judges whether you can do so at their regular meetings as well. You should ask the professionals who are doing psychiatric evaluations which attorneys and judges are open to considering changes to the current system. Find an attorney dealing with a highly conflicted case and ask him or her to consider asking the court to use the services of an evaluator. Don't lose heart: Change does not come easy to the courts. It may take many baby steps to help attorneys and judges see the value of evaluations. But once the ball starts rolling, change can occur quickly. It's just a matter of getting things there.

MYTH #11: ANY COUNSELOR CAN PERFORM CUSTODY EVALUATIONS

Truth #11: Even putting education, training, supervision, and practice aside, not all counselors are suited to be effective custody evaluators. The ideal person must communicate with a wide variety of people; deal with high levels of conflict, including any attendant histrionics and drama; have the ability to set aside negative testimony experiences.

A custody evaluator must have the innate ability to appreciate all types of people—for example, let's start with attorneys. Attorneys seem to think just a little bit differently from others in different professions. This is not necessarily bad: It's just how it is. Attorneys advocate on their client's behalf even when what their client needs is someone to slap him or her with some cold, hard reality. Attorneys are trained to do a job that is often difficult and unrewarding, but through it all they stand by their clients. And yet attorneys can differ. Some attorneys function by a set of internal rules that are relatively inflexible. Working with these attorneys is good: They are timely with any responses, organized, and easy to schedule. Other attorneys, however, are more flexible. They may not respond in a timely manner, may be difficult to schedule, and may not seem very organized. Nonetheless, an evaluator must be able to deal with all kinds.

Some attorneys believe that they know more about what children need than trained professional evaluators do, relying on past cases, their own experiences, and the experiences of family and friends. You must listen to the attorney, then politely and professionally find a way to tell him or her what you know to be true. It is a hard conversation. Some attorneys like to argue and bully evaluators to get their way. But the clever evaluator understands this and stands firm in his or her recommendations, grounded in their rationale. You cannot allow yourself to be overwhelmed by a boisterous attorney, nor should you fall into the trap of ignoring what an attorney has to say. It takes a talented evaluator to walk the fine line between being professional and being hard to work with.

Judges also differ in their approaches to family conflicts. All judges work within the rules of the bench; thus, you can expect a degree of uniformity between judges. But depending on their experiences, their time sitting on the bench, and their faith in evaluators in general, different judges approach their job differently. For example, some judges talk to the child in their chambers regardless of whether the evaluator has interviewed the children. Some judges don't ask questions of the evaluator during testimony; other judges always do. Some judges give attorneys wide leeway in questioning the evaluator, whereas others keep them on a tight leash when it comes to the types of questions asked. Regardless, the judge makes the rules, and a wise evaluator respects that authority.

A good evaluator can deal with high levels of conflict between parents day after day, case after case. Every case is different, but they all share a similarity: The conflict between the parents has taken on a life of its own. At times you will want to scream at the parents to tell them what they need to do. This might be cathartic, but there is a better way. You must appreciate every parent's story while still reading between the lines of that story. You must see through the drama to put together a picture of what is really happening in the family, including the children. As each case ends, you must file it on your shelf and move on to a fresh case with a new family, leaving your baggage behind.

Evaluators often testify in court, particularly at the beginning of their career, before establishing a reputation. Testifying in court isn't fun, but it doesn't have to be painful, either. It takes patience and emotional control, particularly if an attorney asks questions that provoke internal outrage. An attorney might try to fluster an evaluator and make him or her change his or her recommendations as if they were not based on the evaluator's reasoned judgment about the realities of the case. If your recommendations are right, then no attorney should be able to change your mind—but he or she will try anyway. Keep your emotions in check, act professionally, answer succinctly, and don't take anything personally. The attorney is just doing his or her job, advocating on his or her client's behalf. You may like some attorneys better than others, but that doesn't mean it's personal—regardless of your preferences, you can work with any client to do the job of a professional custody evaluator.

You'll probably encounter other myths about evaluation as you work in the family law courts. Some will make you shake your head and wonder. Others will make you angry. But remember your job: to do what it takes to communicate effectively while speaking for the child in family court.

Scope of Practice and Training Standards for Custody Evaluators, Mediators, and Case Managers

By now you have a general understanding of what it means to be a custody evaluator, mediator, or case manager. You understand that none of these jobs is easy or for the faint of heart. It takes a well-trained professional to become an effective evaluator, mediator, or case manager. Now it is time to talk more specifically about the business side, the training side, and the pitfalls and benefits of working with the family court.

GENERAL TRAINING STANDARDS FOR CUSTODY EVALUATORS, MEDIATORS, AND CASE MANAGERS

Educational Requirements: Classes

Training to be a custody evaluator bears discussion in more detail. Let's start with the necessary education. While you are working on graduating with your degree in counseling, think ahead and take classes that may not be required for your degree but that will be important if you want to be effective as a forensic counselor. Take family classes, especially ones that focus on systemic theories. Take classes discussing family issues such as divorce and blended families. Also take classes that focus on family counseling skills. Do at least some of your internship at sites that provide family counseling sessions so that you can practice your family counseling skills with real families who are in conflict. This will also hone your skills in working with more than one client at a time and understanding different perspectives on the same issue.

Additionally, take classes specific to counseling children. These classes should focus on the developmental issues of children of all ages. The classes should also focus on issues of childhood, especially conflict within the family, divorce, and blended families. The classes need to have a component on how to be a play therapist. The skills of a play therapist are most useful when interviewing children during a custody evaluation: It takes a skillful counselor to be able to relate with a child given only minimal time for relationship building. A counselor who has play therapy skills has the advantage of being able to listen to a child's words and understand their underlying meaning. The skills of a play therapist allow the counselor to hear the child and give him or her some hope and some relief from his or her worries and fears of the new and different life ahead. The time spent with an evaluator who has the skills of a play therapist, though brief, will give the child some relief from his or her pain and instill a belief that he or she can withstand the pain and changes in his or her family of origin, thus providing the child a chance to tell his or her story and feel as if he or she has some control of an environment that may well feel totally out of his or her control.

Educational Requirements: Internship

Again, as part of your internship you should find a site that provides opportunities for you to work with children of all ages. The site should also allow you to counsel using play therapy techniques. This will give you both practice and confidence. Included in the internship should be opportunities to practice your counseling skills with older children and adolescents. All the counseling skills you have learned will give you the skills necessary for counseling with children and adolescents. During your internship, you can refine those skills working with children.

Educational Requirements: Professional Developmental Workshops

As a final step, take any workshops or lectures made available through professional development programs or professional conferences. Because you attend professional conferences anyway, take any workshops that will benefit your skills in forensics. State counseling conferences often have at least one workshop dealing with forensic counseling. A national conference, such as the American Counseling Association International Conference, generally has numerous lectures on forensic counseling. These workshops will give you good information to help you improve your abilities as an evaluator and will provide up-to-date information on changes in the family courts in different jurisdictions. These conferences not only are good for reaffirming your professionalism, but also provide a wealth of information to help you maintain your counseling skills, knowledge, and professionalism.

Licensing

Beyond receiving your counseling degree, you must also become licensed in your state. Some states have one license for counselors, who are commonly called licensed professional counselors. Other states have different tiers of license. You must be licensed on the bottom tier first, then spend more supervised hours and pass another exam to be licensed at higher tiers. Your ultimate goal is to be licensed at the top tier. Whatever type of license is available in your state, you must become licensed and then maintain your license. Ultimately, you need to be licensed at the highest tier of license available. There will be times when you will need to testify opposite another evaluator, often one from a different mental health profession. You must be able to compete on a license-to-license basis to prevent attorneys from questioning your recommendations based on your level of professional license. Hold the highest professional license possible, maintain it, and be proud to be a licensed professional counselor.

So now you have your degree in counseling and you hold the appropriate license. Take some time to practice your profession. Work as a counselor in the field. Work with families and children in both group counseling and individual counseling. Meet other professionals, take continuing education classes, and attend professional workshops and conferences. Keep your eyes open for other counselors who are working as evaluators, mediators, or case managers. Introduce yourself to family law attorneys and judges. Build professional relationships with such people so that when you are ready for supervision as an evaluator, mediator, or case manager you will know to whom to turn for training and support. Become the best counselor you can be, and then seek out supervision so that you can become the best evaluator you can be.

If you already hold your counseling degree and license, you will need to further educate yourself about the world of forensic counseling, specifically about being a custody evaluator, mediator, or case manager. Read books and articles. Go to professional workshops and conferences offering educational sessions in forensic counseling. Begin to establish relationships with counselors who are already working in the field. Hone your counseling skills by working with families and children of all ages. Fill in all the blanks you have concerning working with children of all ages and families. You already know how to do this, because you previously sought information about issues your clients have brought to the table about which you had little information. Start doing this now: Practice and refine your skills.

Supervision

The next important step is receiving supervision from an evaluator, mediator, or case manager. You have most likely already developed relationships with professionals who are doing these jobs, so now you need their supervision and mentorship. Try to receive supervision from a person who has many evaluations, mediations, or case management cases under his or her belt. Try to pick a supervisor who is highly thought of in the family courts and who has a reputation for doing a good job from both attorneys and judges' perspectives. Find a supervisor who holds a similar license to your own and, if possible, who has received training in supervision theory and skills.

Some jurisdictions require you to have had at least some supervised cases. Indeed, it is in your best interest to receive as much supervision as possible. This will only improve your work performance and your reputation as a high-quality evaluator, mediator, or case manager. In the future, it will also provide you with someone to consult about cases. Everyone working in the field of forensics needs someone with whom to consult to understand the intricacies of high-conflict cases.

Start your supervision by watching the process unfold. Take notes, listen carefully, and reflect on what you like about the process as well as what you would change. All evaluators, mediators, and case managers do their work in slightly different ways, and you will be no different. Take what you like and include it. Discard methods you don't like. Modify the process to fit your skills and counseling style. You can use guidelines, but you can also change them to better suit you. So watch, learn, and listen. Ask questions of your supervisor to help you understand what he or she is doing with the parents and the children and why.

After you have observed a complete evaluation, mediation, or case, take on a case while the supervisor watches you. The supervisor will point out when you might have missed something or done something that didn't work. He or she will also ask you why you did what you did, and vice versa. A good supervisor will also point out your strengths and abilities. This is when you learn how to become the best forensic counselor you can be. Remember what it was like in your graduate program when you received supervision from faculty: There were times you walked out after a supervision session certain you would never get the whole counseling thing. There were other times when you felt you actually could become a counselor. You will have the same feelings after these supervision sessions. The good thing is you already know how to be an effective counselor. All you have to learn is how to use your skills to become an effective evaluator, mediator, or case manager. It takes time, but pity those evaluators who were first in this job. They had to struggle along without support or guidance, discovering for themselves what worked, what didn't work, and what most helped the judge issue orders to meet the best interests of the child. It was much like walking in a dark room trying to find the light switch. This is now a struggle that you don't have to go through alone. Even working under a supervisor will not always be easy, but it is a lot better than the alternative.

Additional Training Requirements: Mediator

Becoming a mediator or case manager takes the same dedication to education, practice, and supervision. There are some differences in the additional training and supervision required to become a qualified mediator. Mediator training is often provided by the courts, since mediators are used more often than evaluators or case managers. Contact Court Services to receive notice of future training sessions and to find out how to be put on the qualified mediator list, the rotation used by the courts.

As you recall, the mediator's work is different from that of an evaluator. Mediators work with the parents, not the children. They also work with the parents together, not the parents separately. They do not listen to the parents give their individual perspectives on what has happened to end the family, but rather listen to the parents explain what they cooperatively think would work best to eliminate conflict in the future and be best for the child's future positive growth. Mediation is more like a business deal than the emotional interviews with the evaluator. The mediation session helps find compromise between the parents and allows the parents to agree on how they will dissolve the family. The agreement includes both custody and visitation and property division. As you recall, custody evaluations do not deal with property division. Nonetheless, mediators need to understand the value of property and how it might be divided, as well as the state's community property laws. Furthermore, they need to know the guidelines for child support and spousal support.

Classes are available to teach mediation skills. Take as many as you can until you have a firm understanding of what mediation is and is not. A mediator's job is to keep the emotion out of the discussions and keep the parents focused on conversations that facilitate compromise and agreement about custody, visitation, and property division. The parents may want to tell their individual stories or argue with each other over sometimes meaningless things. It is the mediator's job to help the parents understand that spending hundreds of dollars an hour arguing over canning jars or a charcoal barbeque is beyond ridiculous. The mediator needs to bring reality into the sessions and keep the parents on track to agree on property division and the custody and visitation schedule.

The skills of a counselor also come into play for a mediator. The mediator should be cognizant of the power differential between the parents. Mediation only works if both participants come into the session on an equal power standing. One parent cannot hold power over the other. One parent cannot bully the other to get his or her way. It is the mediator's job to rein in the parent who is taking control of the session and make sure that both parents have equal time to talk and explain their positions. Just as it is the mediator's job to keep the conversation on a businesslike and mostly unemotional level, it is also his or her job to make sure that each parent has the time to talk and be heard by the other parent.

Additional Training Requirements: Case Manager

A case manager is a professional who primarily does the job of a mediator or a custody evaluator but who also occasionally does the work of a case manager. Not many do the job of case manager exclusively. This is a job for a person who combines unlimited patience with a tolerance for the ridiculous and absurd. A case manager is like a parent to the parents, because the parents can't get along and often act like children rather than coparenting adults.

The case manager's job is to listen to both parents' concerns and then decide how to resolve the conflict. For example, one parent might contact the case manager to tell how the other parent is always late at exchanges. The "late" parent says that he or she isn't late and counters that the other parent is early and so of course has to wait a long time. The case manager decides on a 20-minute cushion at exchanges. If the other parent is not there to receive the child within the 20-minute time frame, then the visitation is cancelled. These types of complaints happen regularly, even daily, over and over again. Thus, it is essential for the case manager to be patient with and tolerant of these kinds of issues, as well as immune to continued whining and complaining from the parents.

The training required to become a case manager is similar to that for a custody evaluator. The case manager needs knowledge of the child's developmental needs and works in the child's best interest. He or she must also be able to listen to the parents' words and hear the underlying emotions. The case manager consults with the evaluator and occasionally the mediator, but must be able to know when he or she is being manipulated and triangulated between the parents and avoid those situations. He or she must have learned and practiced establishing not only his or her own boundaries but also boundaries for others. He or she must be able to speak clearly and explicitly and to confront appropriately.

THE BUSINESS DECISIONS OF BEING AN EVALUATOR, MEDIATOR, OR CASE MANAGER

Most forensic counselors tend to choose to be either an evaluator or mediator and then decide whether they want to be a case manager occasionally. Usually the person decides which direction he or she wants his or her practice to go and becomes exceptional in that arena. Finances can also push the forensic counselor in one direction or another. The business end of being a forensic counselor is sometimes overlooked, but it, too, needs to be considered and understood.

Getting Paid

Being a forensic counselor is hard work, and it takes time. None of the work of an evaluator, mediator, or case manager can be billed through insurance companies, so it is a cash business. Payment is due before the work begins and cannot be paid in installments. What you charge depends on where you live and how much other forensic counselors in the area are charging. Check with others in your area to find out how much they charge and how they expect to receive payment. Usually, you'll charge a flat rate to conduct an evaluation that culminates in rec-ommendations provided to the court. Mediation is generally billed by the session, since some people can finish their mediated agreement in one session whereas others take longer to agree. Case management cases generally see money held in an account from which money is drawn each time the case manager has contact with either party. Find out how others in your area deal with the financial end of this business, and fol-low suit. You may find that you want to modify your billing practices as time goes on, but whatever you do, make sure you are paid before you begin working.

Billing Options: Custody Evaluators

Custody evaluators generally bill a flat rate based on a minimum of four appointments, collateral contacts, report writing, and consultation with the attorneys. Figure your hourly rate for an approximately 8-hour minimum, then find out what others in your profession and your area are charging. You don't want to undercut other evaluators, nor do you want to overcharge and never be asked to do an evaluation. In figuring your rate, remember how much attorneys are charging clients by the hour—you are worth something at least approaching that. You are not going to become rich doing evaluations, but you need to be compen-sated for the professional work you are doing. When you finally decide on a reasonable flat rate, your first thought may be that it seems too high. It isn't too high. Remember that the parents can stop this process any time they choose to get along and become the coparents they need to be for their child.

You also need to establish what you are going to charge for updated reports. Updates generally take less time than the original evaluation, but not always. It is reasonable to establish a flat rate for an updated report and then establish an hourly rate for any time after, say, 4 hours. Whatever you establish, be sure it is consistent between all cases.

Evaluations are court-ordered and encompass how your fee will be paid. Generally, the cost of the evaluation is split equally between the parents. Therefore, on the day of the parents' first appointment, each parent must bring his or her half of the fee in full to the appointment. Cash, money orders, or personal checks are acceptable methods of payment. Some evaluators may take credit cards, but most do not. Additionally, some evaluators do not take personal checks. If a parent asks to make payments, say no. If the parent asks to pay on the second appointment, say no. If the parent asks to pay half now and half at the second appointment, say no. Agree to set the first appointment later after the parent has saved the full amount and can pay you then. This is a business; you expect to be paid. You must be paid in advance—if one of the parents doesn't like your conclusions, he or she might not pay you. Get your money first; don't feel sorry for a parent and abandon your business plan for him or her. Remember: The parents are the ones who have behaved in such a way as to make an evaluation necessary. Accordingly, they get to pay for your services.

Once you have established the flat rate for an evaluation, establish your hourly rate for court testimony and travel time to court. Court testimony is billed by the hour, generally at the rate the attorney is getting paid for work in court. It is paid by the party who requests that you appear in court and testify about your recommendations. The hourly rate for court testimony begins when you step foot inside the courthouse. If you are left sitting in the hall, you are still getting paid. If you show up to court and are told you aren't needed, bill for your time nevertheless. Some evaluators charge half their hourly testifying rate for time spent waiting; others charge the full amount. Some evaluators who are sent home upon arriving charge half their hourly rate; others charge the full rate. Regardless, the attorney who requested your testimony should be able to tell you when to be at court, ready to testify, and not waste your time with sitting and waiting. Remember, attorneys are charging their clients the same way. You should be treated no differently.

Travel time is also paid by the hour. If court is in the same town as your practice, generally no travel cost is attendant. If court is out of the town where you practice, then establish the rate you charge for travel.

Some evaluators charge by the mile at the going rate for reimbursement by the IRS. Others charge by the hour from their office to the out-of-town courthouse. If you charge by the hour, you might want to halve your hourly rate for testimony and charge that amount per hour for travel.

Because you won't know how long your testimony will be, you can't be paid prior to testimony. Therefore, the cost of testimony and travel is charged to the attorney who requests your presence in court. Tell the attorney your rates for testimony and travel and give him or her an approximate total. Encourage him or her to collect money for paying your bill from the client prior to your testimony so that he or she can pay your bill in a timely fashion. On rare occasions, you will have to bill the attorney twice to get paid. You may have to call the attorney and remind him or her to pay your bill, although this rarely happens. Never give up on getting paid. You worked for the money, you did your job, and you deserve to get paid. Counselors are notorious for being poor businesspeople, but that doesn't have to be true of you. Always be clear and up front about your costs, and always get paid for your work. Make being paid your mission if you have to.

Last, remember that refunds never happen. Make it very clear to both parents that after they pay and begin the process, you give neither refunds nor partial refunds. On very rare occasions, one parent may be ordered to pay the full amount of the evaluation. Schedule that parent first so that you are paid before doing any of the evaluation. If after that one appointment a settlement is reached, refund half the amount paid. Whatever your policy on refunds and payments, be crystal clear about every one of your expectations regarding payment, type of payment, and refund policy. Also be clear that you cannot and will not bill insurance companies for your services as an evaluator.

Billing Options: Mediators

Mediators set an hourly or per-session rate and then set the length of time for a session. Sessions are generally 2 to 3 hours long, so figure your hourly rate and then contact other mediators and find out what they charge. It will generally be more than your hourly rate as a therapist. Being a mediator is hard work, so don't undercut yourself. Some mediators take payment at the beginning of the session, whereas others take payment at its end. Getting paid before the session is best; at that point, neither parent is worked up or angry about the outcome of the session and thus reluctant to pay. Just always remember that you run a business—handle payment in a businesslike fashion.

Billing Options: Case Managers

Case managers take a retainer from each parent once ordered by the court to manage the case. The retainer should be large enough to cover numerous contacts per month. You have to make guess how many contacts will happen each week. A good estimate is two contacts weekly. Then set a rate per contact. Remember that some contacts will take little time; others will take more. Figure at least half your hourly rate as a therapist for each contact. Many case managers charge their full hourly rate for a contact if they have to spend more than half an hour responding to the issue. If they spend less time responding, they charge half their hourly rate. Check with others who have been case managers and find out what they charged for their services. Whatever you charge, be clear to both parents how you will bill the retainer. Your billing has to reflect the date of the contact, the length of service, and the cost associated with that contact. Also decide how low the amount of the retainer can fall before the parents have to pay into it again. Generally, when the retainer has only a quarter of the original fund, the case manager requires payment from both parents again.

Case managers also have to decide how the parents can contact them. Many prefer to be contacted by e-mail, others by telephone. Whichever method is used, respond in a timely fashion to the parent's concern. This is generally done within 24 hours if not before. You must be committed to quickly and decisively returning phone calls and answering e-mails. You also have to make it clear to both parents that they, too, must read their e-mails daily and respond to phone calls within a specified time limit. The job of a case manager is to mitigate conflict quickly so that it doesn't take on a life of its own. Not responding quickly to a parent's concern allows the issue to grow and ultimately become unmanageable. The case manager is dealing with parents who have abandoned their responsibility to get along with the other parent and who have abdicated their responsibility to make decisions that are in the child's best interest to the case manager. Thus, the case manager needs to make decisions and help the parents resolve their conflicts in a timely manner. Your billing sheet needs to be readily available to both parents, and provided to them without fail each month.

CHALLENGES AND REWARDS OF BEING
A FORENSIC COUNSELOR

At this point you may be wondering why anyone would want to be a forensic counselor. The work is hard, and you won't get rich doing it. Dealing with people who are in high levels of conflict and who seem to be unable to break the cycle of disharmony is not work suited to everyone. Mediating property distribution and custody and visitation schedules between two people who hold intense hostility toward each other is certainly not easy and stress-free. A forensic counselor knows that he or she is never going to make everyone happy—at least one parent will not like his or her conclusions. This concept is hard for counselors to wrap their heads around; counselors, by their nature, are helpful people and are trained to provide opportunities for clients to make their own choices and decisions. The role of the forensic counselor is not the traditional role of a counselor.

So as you have seen there are difficult aspects to this job. But there are also great rewards. It is truly rewarding to speak for the child. No one else speaks for the child but you: The parents, for example, speak from their standpoint, and the attorneys speak as an advocate for their clients. If a child has a personal counselor, that person speaks from a therapeutic point of view. A teacher speaks from the child's academic world. A child care provider speaks from that arena. No one but the evaluator speaks for the child from the child's own experience to the court. Thanks to the evaluator, someone is watching out and standing up for the child without an agenda other than what is in the child's best interests.

Another reward of an evaluator's job is providing the parents with a forum for telling their stories to an unbiased professional. The evaluator provides the opportunity for each parent to speak from his or her perspective to someone who is trained in listening. The parent can come to understand where this case is headed and what he or she can do differently, and identify incongruencies in his or her story and beliefs. Most importantly, however, the parent has someone to listen to him or her and hear what he or she has to say. It is very rare for a parent to leave an interview with an evaluator feeling worse than when he or she came into the office; rather, the parent typically leaves feeling better for having had the opportunity to tell his or her story. It is therapeutic to have someone listen with a professional ear.

It is also rewarding to work with the attorneys and judges who are involved in family law cases. These people are committed to doing what is right and what is in the best interest of the child. They may approach the case from a different angle than the evaluator does, but they genuinely want to do what is best for the child. Educating the attorneys and judges about the child's developmental needs and the realities of this particular case, as well as helping them understand the entire case from an evaluator's perspective is also rewarding. The attorneys and judges are mostly grateful to have the assistance of an evaluator, mediator, or case manager in these high-conflict cases. They may not admit it, but it often seems that they know they are in too deep for their expertise—they need help from someone who knows what he or she is doing when it comes to this type of case.

Finally, it is rewarding to know that you made a difference in a child's life. It is possible you have made a difference in the parents' lives as well. The chances of you ever finding out how the child grows and develops are slim to none, but, as in counseling, you must have faith that you made a positive difference. Occasionally a parent or one of the attorneys will tell you how the court resolved the case. This doesn't happen very often, and it is rare that an evaluator will seek out this information. A mediator knows how the session went and whether there was a resolution. A case manager knows whether the number of complaints drops and whether the parents are trying to settle their differences between themselves without the aid of the case manager. The evaluator works in faith that his or her work made a positive difference for a child. This work is as rewarding as it is hard.

5

Ethical Considerations for Custody Evaluators, Mediators, and Case Managers

Understanding the ethical code of your profession is a must. Functioning within the guidelines of an ethical code is what licensed professional practitioners do in their professional and personal lives. Being a professional person means also being an ethical person. There is no reason to belabor the various ethical codes, such as the American Counseling Association Ethical Code; being a professional counselor, you have already studied the codes applicable to you. Whatever mental health professions you belong to, you know and understand their codes of ethics. Furthermore, you practice within the codes that apply to you and make ethical decisions—and remember that many licenses require a continuing education course on ethics each year.

Working as a forensic counselor does not relieve you from also being an ethical counselor. However, some of your ethical considerations will be inherently different when working as an evaluator, mediator, or case manager. The code still guides your practice, but because of the public nature of legal cases, some things are different for a forensic counselor.

CONFIDENTIALITY

One of the cornerstones of any ethical code is confidentiality. Without confidentiality, no therapeutic relationship would exist. Counselors guard confidentiality in their practice. They explain what confidentiality means to their clients. They also explain under what circumstances they could be forced to break confidentiality. Much of the intake session is devoted to talking about confidentiality and the boundaries surrounding it. But for a custody evaluator, case manager, or mediator, the concept of confidentiality takes on a slightly different hue.

People who choose to put their issues in the hands of the legal system are also choosing to put their issues in the public arena. Legal cases are public, not confidential, though some aspects of a case may be ordered sealed from the public eye. Cases in the family law court are considered public information. Even the results of such cases are published in the local newspaper. Therefore, confidentiality is not an issue except in certain circumstances, such as when a judge so orders and within the sphere of attorney–client privilege. The work of the forensic counselor is not considered confidential—except for the work of mediators and work done during mediation. An evaluator does not have the responsibility to maintain confidentiality in his or her work for the courts. This concept is very hard to accept as a licensed professional counselor, but get used to it: Confidentiality is not an issue for an evaluator or a case manager.

That said, a good evaluator does not blatantly violate confidentiality. You must find a middle ground between guarding the confidentiality of your client and "telling all" about your case. As an evaluator, you have to make a paradigm shift when it comes to confidentiality. You have to find a place of peace that allows you to protect some degree of confidentiality while knowing that your work will ultimately become public knowledge. In other words, you must know when to talk and when to keep your mouth closed.

The parents and children in a custody evaluation case are not your therapeutic clients. They have been ordered to appear in your office and (in the case of the parents) to pay for the services you ultimately provide to the court. You hope to help the parents better understand their situation and make different choices in order to improve their child's life both during and after the divorce, but the work that you do as an evaluator is the property of the legal system. It is not the property of the parents, the attorneys, or even the judge. Your work is the property of all these people because it is potentially the property of the public. Thus, your job is to accept that what you do as an evaluator is not confidential—and yet to not talk about your work to just anybody. This conflict can be a minefield for the evaluator: You try to maintain confidentiality, knowing that it may turn out to be impossible.

At the first sessions, be very clear to each parent about the lack of confidentiality in the evaluation process. In addition, tell each parent that you will try to maintain confidentiality throughout the process but emphasize that doing so might not be possible. The parents or child must understand that you are not going to abuse the lack of confidentiality—but that likewise you cannot protect confidentiality as you could if you had a therapeutic relationship with the parent or the child. Make sure that the parent clearly understands that what he or she says to you may well be brought up in a public forum, and that no assumption of confidentiality covers what is discussed. Many times the parent thinks that time spent with you is subject to the same parameters of confidentiality as time spent with an attorney or a therapist. It is not—this must be made crystal clear.

The parent also needs to understand at the first session that you will not keep secrets from the other parent. That does not mean that you will tell the other parent everything, but neither is it your job to side with one parent over the other; accordingly, you will not conceal information relevant to the evaluation process. Likewise, you will not be a party to untruths. You will tell the truth even when it is hard for a parent or child to hear. You will not sugarcoat the truth, and you will not conceal the truth when it needs to be told. One of the reasons the parents are getting a divorce is because they weren't honest and straightforward with each other. You will not do that to either of them.

Last, make it clear to both parents that you are not an attorney and thus cannot give them legal advice. You can tell them what might happen and explain what some legal terms mean, but you cannot give legal advice. Likewise, you cannot make promises about the outcome of the evaluation or the court order. Being involved in the legal system is always a gamble. The outcome can never be known for sure ahead of time, and making promises about the outcome is a terrible mistake on an evaluator's part. Explain that you may form an opinion about what the outcome of this case will be, but you can never say anything for sure.

DUAL RELATIONSHIPS

Another area of the ethics code concerns dual relationships. You must decide what your role will be in this particular case. Decide before you begin whether you are going to be the evaluator, mediator, or case manager. You can't be everything for every case. Generally, forensic counselors decide what area of emphasis they will provide for the courts and stay within that arena. If you are an evaluator, then be only an evaluator; follow the same principle for mediation and case management. For example, if you take a case as a mediator, you cannot jump over to being the evaluator if the mediation fails. If you are the evaluator for a case and a case manager is ordered, it is best that you not be the case manager. However, if you have completed an evaluation and the court orders an update of the evaluation, it makes sense for you to continue with the case and do the update of your own original evaluation.

Of course, if you know any of the participants in a case, you cannot take the case as an evaluator, mediator, or case manager. Likewise, if you have a therapeutic relationship with any of the parties of a case, you cannot take on any role as a forensic counselor. You can assist the evaluator by consulting about your role as the counselor, but you cannot be involved by switching roles to be the evaluator, mediator, or case manager.

PAYMENT

Bartering is not acceptable as a form of payment for the services of a forensic counselor. Payment is in cash. Some clients will say that they don't have the money to pay for the evaluation, the mediation, or the retainer for a case manager, but that they can provide you with a service. You have to deal with this dilemma from a business standpoint by telling the parent that you must be paid in cash or will be unable to take the case. You might need a new roof on your house, but it's money or nothing for your services. If the recommendations are not what the roofer wants, you may well get no roof or only part of a roof. Take only money—always.

THERAPEUTIC RELATIONSHIP

Working for the courts as a forensic counselor is not the same as being a counselor working as a therapist. Make it clear from the first session that your job is not to do therapy any more than it is to try to reunite the parents. Establishing a therapeutic relationship is not within the purview of an evaluator, mediator, or case manager. You must establish a working relationship with the parent or child to have a successful interview. Even so, these sessions are not therapy; rather, they are interviews in which you gain information necessary to making reasonable recommendations. A working relationship is also necessary for a successful mediation outcome and essential to resolving conflicts successfully as a case manager. You should use the skills of a therapist to establish this working relationship, but you make it crystal clear that you are not going to engage in actual therapy.

Certainly there will be times during the interview when you use counseling skills such as reflections or summaries to better understand what the parent or child is trying to tell you. The interviews are generally emotional for both parents and the child. It is difficult talking about the breakup of a family from both the adults' and child's perspectives. Be understanding and respectful of the parents' and child's feelings, but not to the level you would be as the parents' or child's counselor. The sessions that occur during an evaluation are often therapeutic for the parent or child, but this is because you were a good listener and understood his or her side of the story; it is always therapeutic to tell one's story to someone who is unbiased and impartial. Giving a parent or child a sense of your understanding is a good thing, but it is not therapy. The chief similarity between what you do and therapy is that in both cases you keep notes about each session. However, you also keep notes for every contact intersecting the case.

RECORD KEEPING

Record keeping is something you must do well. During your interviews with the parents, take notes as they talk. With practice, you will be able to write while holding a conversation. Your notes are your lifeline, helping you remember what each parent talked about during his or her session. Notes are also vital records of your time with the child. Make notes of the session with the child immediately after it ends. Your notes may reflect actual statements but should at least comprise the gist of what was said during the session. Your notes also describe incongruencies in what was said and include a timeline of events and concerns that you need to come to better understand. Your notes are your recollection of what was said. Do not expect to remember what each parent said and what the child told you without making a note of it. Your notes should be written in such a way that when you read them later they put you right back into the session they record.

Mediators and case managers also keep notes about their contacts with the parents. The mediator's notes reflect the issues the parents bring to the mediation as well as the ultimate outcome and remediation of these issues. Case managers keep notes of the contacts initiated by either parent and by the case manager. These notes not only denote the issue brought forward, but also assist in the billing process.

Just as your sessions as an evaluator are not confidential, neither are your notes. Often the attorneys will ask to look at your notes or to make copies of them. If you have written the truth of what happened during the session without bias, this is of no concern to you. The attorneys may not understand all your shorthand marks, but that is their problem, not yours. (Some shorthand marks may be arrows pointing to specific things you wrote, either denoting an incongruency or something that needs your attention, or stars, perhaps meaning "pay attention to this.") Regardless of what system you use, it should be at least generally understandable to another reader, such as an attorney. If you don't have notes, the attorneys will break out into huge smiles thinking about how poorly you will do during court testimony and, conversely, how good they will look during it.

Likewise, a case manager's notes are not confidential. The court or the attorneys can request copies of the case manager's notes just as they can for those of an evaluator. However, the mediator's notes are confidential and are not available to the court or either attorney. Because the mediation process is confidential, so are the notes generated during the sessions.

Record Storage

The length of time you should store your notes is difficult to determine. Some evaluators keep all their notes for all their cases forever. Some choose to destroy notes older than 5 years. However long you choose to keep your notes, it is important that you understand the developmental nature of these types of custody cases. After cases are initially settled, there tends to be a hiatus from the legal system. However, there is also a developmental aspect to these cases as well. Modifications tend to occur when the child begins kindergarten, reaches the age of 10 to 12, and gets a driver's license. At these turning points in a child's life, the visitation schedule may no longer fits the child's needs and best interests. For example, if a young child has a visitation schedule that includes a midweek overnight when he or she enters kindergarten, this may not be appropriate for the child's academic success: A change may need to be made to the visitation schedule. When a child turns 10, 11, or 12, he or she begins to have a social life that includes overnights on the weekends with friends, a time when the child may have visitation. Also, the child may play in extracurricular games on the weekends, and that, too, may not fit a particular visitation schedule. When the child gets his or her driver's license, he or she becomes more independent and is often reluctant to continue abiding by a structured visitation schedule. In other words, when the child gets his or her driver's license, all bets are off for a visitation schedule that doesn't include the child's input.

Because many of these cases will require modifications and the parents still can't cooperate with each other to make such modifications without outside intervention, the judge will often make an order for an updated evaluation by the original evaluator. If you have destroyed the notes from the original evaluation, you must begin again. If you kept the notes, you can reread them, remember the case, and start the update from the present time. You will be amazed how often you need to go to your filing cabinet and pull the notes from an old case because it is back in the system again.

So how long should you keep your old case notes? If you have the room, keep all of them forever. If you don't have the room, keep them for at least 5 years. Although they aren't confidential, when you destroy them be sure to shred them, not just put them in the trash. However, if you are a mediator, any notes are confidential and should be treated accordingly. In your role as mediator you will probably take notes only to give everyone continuity between sessions. After an agreement is signed, your notes can be destroyed. If the mediation fails and the judge has been notified of the failure, your notes can also be destroyed. A case manager keeps brief notes about each contact not only to bill the retainer correctly, but also to track the types of conflicts that keep recurring. After your job as the case manager is finished and the money has been settled, you can destroy your notes, but the billing should be maintained for several years.

DO NO HARM

Finally, you have the ethical responsibility to do no harm to your clients. Of course you will not attempt to harm any of the people that you are evaluating, mediating, or managing, but rarely are both parents happy with the outcome. Generally at least one parent feels angry, misunderstood, and "harmed" by your recommendations or decisions. Remember: Your voice is the child's voice in court. You work for the child and his or her best interest, not in support of what the parents want or think they need. Also remember that you are working with people who have taken the conflict between them to a new level. The parents can stop this process any time simply by getting along and coparenting effectively. You cannot keep everyone happy all the time no matter your role. You at least have a shot at two happy parents if the parents agree on a settlement. But if the mediation fails, the result will be two unhappy parents.

Therefore, although you don't set out to harm the parents or the child and do not make recommendations or decisions in an attempt to do harm, the parents or child may feel as if that is what has happened nevertheless. If you do the job the court hires you to do in a professional, unbiased way that reflects your training, then you have done your job even if the end result leaves the parents feeling misunderstood and even harmed. You have read it before, but read it again: It takes a certain type of person to be an evaluator, mediator, or case manager. Specifically, it takes a counselor who does not take parents' feelings of anger to heart.

As a licensed professional counselor, you will continue to abide by the ethical standards of your profession. As a forensic licensed professional counselor, you will have to balance the licensed professional counselor's code with the new reality and needs of your new job, understanding the difference between a counselor who does therapy with clients and a counselor who works for the court. Continue to make ethical decisions, and when in doubt, consult with another professional forensic counselor before acting. You are a reasonable person and counselor—you can do this.

6

Interviewing Basics

It's time to begin interviewing the parents and children. There are some basic guidelines to follow, but remember: These are guidelines, not hard-and-fast rules. You will change and supplement these guidelines to better match them to your skill set and traits. You won't find out exactly what works for you until you have completed several evaluations. Even then, you will modify your usual way of interviewing for some cases. If you use standardized assessments, schedule time for the parent to take the assessments before the interview. Choose any assessments carefully: Be sure they will give you information that helps you reach your conclusions. But be aware that no assessment will tell you which parent is the better parent, although it may give you a probable diagnosis. Nonetheless, a diagnosis generally will not be sufficient grounds to restrict contact between the parent and child; as a result, the parent remains the parent and will probably maintain some contact with the child. Also, you will find that generally assessments end up taking time and money while giving little in return.

INTERVIEWS: GENERAL PROCEDURE

At minimum, you will interview both of the parents once, separately, for about 2 hours apiece. Try to schedule the parents' appointments prior to sessions with the child. You will also conduct a session with each of the parents separately with their child, lasting approximately

30 to 45 minutes. Additionally, you will have a session with the child alone, for a duration depending on the child's age and ability to communicate with you. Generally, this session also will be about 30 to 45 minutes. In addition, you will get in touch with appropriate collateral contacts. Ultimately you will write recommendations for the court regarding custody and visitation arrangements to serve the best interest of the child.

PARENT INTERVIEWS

The session with each parent is where the evaluator begins to understand the issues of the case. It is during these interviews when each parent gets to tell the evaluator what happened in the past, what is happening now, and what he or she thinks would work best for the child with regard to custody and visitation. This time is when you begin to understand the case in terms of parenting skills, communication skills, emotional involvement, flexibility, caregiving, and potential ability to coparent. The session with the parent has six basic phases.

Phase 1

First, introduce the evaluation process and explain what it is and is not. The parent must understand the boundaries on confidentiality, as well as what you are going to do and how you go about writing your recommendations to the court. At this time, you will discuss payment and how the money the parent is paying will be used. You will also discuss any additional costs, including for court testimony and travel. Often the parent wants to get started right away, so you might discuss money at the end of the session, when the parent is paying your fee and you are writing your receipt.

Most parents are nervous when they come to your office. They know that your recommendations are important to the court and thus can be very persuasive with the judge. They are anxious because they don't know what to expect from you or the conversation they are about to have. At this point, your counseling skills are especially important. Make each parent feel comfortable enough to talk with you freely and honestly. He or she must know that you are hearing him or her—really *listening*. Each parent needs to believe that you understand his or her feelings and torment about the breakup of the family, as well as his or her fears about his or her changing role in the child's life. Use your counseling skills to communicate to each parent that you understand where he or she is coming from. Establish a working relationship with each parent so that he or she will feel free to talk with you about his or her life, the difficulties he or she is experiencing, and his or her fears and frustrations surrounding the legal system and the breakup of the family.

Phase 2

The second phase of the interview is talking about the parent's past with the other parent. A good way to start the conversation is to ask the parent when the two married, how they met, what attracted them, and what they expected from the relationship. Discover the parent's role in the family. Was it as moneymaker? As decision maker? As the supporter? As the emotional one? Talk about how the relationship was at the beginning and how it began to change, then ultimately fail. Discuss the breakup and how the parents decided to deal with their child. Did they agree to a visitation schedule at the breakup, or did they do nothing to maintain contact between both parents and the child? Who stayed in the family home? Who controlled the money after the breakup? How was the child supported after the breakup? Were there other people involved before or directly after the breakup? What other people seem to be "stirring the pot" now? Find out the degree to which each parent tried to keep the child's life constant. Did the parent move often? Did the parent ask the child to change schools or become part of a new family?

With these questions, you are trying to find out the depth of the emotional attachment between the parents and how much remains between them. You are looking for who each parent thought of first before and after the breakup. Did he or she think of his or her own personal happiness and comfort, or of the child's? You want to know if a particular parent is a drama queen, overly unemotional and rational, or carrying emotions that are hindering his or her ability to take care not only of himself or herself but also the child. You want to understand how each parent communicated with the other parent before the breakup and directly after the breakup, and how each parent is doing so now. The level of communication between the parents is telling about how well they can control themselves and what their possible motives are. Is it revenge they seek? Power over the other? To "win" at any cost? Remember that the parents aren't going to outright tell you if they want their counterpart to drop off the face of the earth—but they often do want exactly that. Therefore, you want to begin estimating the emotional stability of each parent, particularly as it relates to his or her relationship with the other parent and the child.

Don't just ask one scripted question after another. Instead, have a conversation with each parent, asking questions when you need to, making supportive statements, and listening carefully. Each parent will tell you what you need to know if you approach him or her correctly. Listen with your counseling ear, and you will hear the incongruencies, inconsistencies, and emotions inside the parent. Remember to make notes during the conversation. Record the timeline of the family from its beginning to its breakup. Also write down each parent's version of his or her relationship with the other parent and how it evolved into the relationship as it stands today. These notes will remind you of the parent's particular perspective and how his or her story differs from the other parent's.

Understanding the past is important, but don't let past events dictate your professional judgments. What happened in the past is important, but even more important is what is happening now. Look for patterns to see whether past behaviors are being recycled into current behaviors. More likely, what happened in the past is not happening now to the same degree. For example, right after the breakup, perhaps the father went out drinking and partying with many women, really living it up as a bachelor. Maybe he maintained contact with the child but didn't behave as he had when the family was intact. As time passed, he realized that all the drinking and partying was taking a toll on his health, his life, and his relationship with his child and former wife. Now he still goes to the bar and has a few drinks, and he dates a variety of women, but his degree of enthusiasm for the bachelor lifestyle has diminished. During the interview, the former wife may want to talk mostly about how he was—not how he is now. It is your job to move the interview forward to understand the father's parenting now and into the future. However, you will interview parents who cannot move beyond what happened in the past. These parents cannot let go of perceived wrongs and instead live their lives in the past, not in the present looking forward to the future. These parents would certainly benefit from regular counseling, and your recommendations should reflect that.

Equally disturbing is the parent who can't understand what the past teaches. These parents can tell you what happened in the past, but they don't learn from it. A woman's former husband was an alcoholic and was prone to domestic violence; her current boyfriend is a drug addict and has been arrested for assault. Not only does this parent fail to understand the poor choices she makes when it comes to relationships, but she also cannot or will not understand how these choices are harmful to the child. Again, your recommendations should include counseling services to help this parent.

To recap, listen to the past, but don't let the past rule your decisions. Compare how things were and how they are now. Are the parents parenting better now than in the past? Are the parents more concerned about their own personal happiness now than they were in the past? Has the glow worn off being the wronged parent and has the drudgery of being a single parent set in? Is there more resentment or less toward the other parent? Is the communication between the parents more effective now than before, or has it broken down over time? These are the things you are listening for during the interview. Thank goodness you have the listening skills of a counselor to assist you.

Phase 3

The third phase is understanding, in detail, what the parent's life is like now. Ask whether he or she is working and, if so, what his or her work schedule is by time and day. Ask whether the other parent is working and determine that parent's work schedule. Ask about child care, including the child's schedule. If the child is in school, ask where, in what grade, and under whose care after school. Next, you need to know about the parent's living situation. Ask where he or she lives, whether he or she rents or owns, and the size of the house. Find out what other people are living with the parent. Find out the number of bedrooms and who sleeps where. The parent who has the child the majority of the time must have the appropriate space for the child or at least a plan for making appropriate space. For example, if the parent is living in a one-bedroom apartment and the child has no room of his or her own, this might be a problem. If the parent plans to get a bigger apartment but is currently unemployed, this also poses a problem. If the parent is living with another person who also has children and there isn't enough room for all the children and the adults, that's another potential problem. If the child has to sleep on a couch because the parent lives with his or her own parents, this could be yet another problem. Everyone needs space and privacy and somewhere he or she can put his or her belongings, a place to feel safe and at home. If the parent cannot provide this type of environment for the child, then this is a concern. It will probably not be the deciding factor, but it is certainly a factor. Remember: You are painting a picture of this parent's life and how the child fits into it. The living situation does not have to be perfect, but it has to be adequate to meet both the parent's needs and the child's.

Ask the parent to tell you about what he or she does in his or her life when not working. What are his or her interests and activities? What does he or she do with the child for fun? If he or she does nothing for fun with his or her child but play video games, or if he or she works out every evening in the gym while the child waits at home, that could be a problem. You are looking to see how involved the parent is in the child's life and to what extent the parent's activities supersede his or her time with the child. Is the parent's setup about his or her personal happiness, or does it include the child's happiness as well? If the parent has the child on weekends but goes out with friends regularly on those weekends, leaving the child with a child care provider, that tells you something about the parent and whose needs he or she is putting first. Likewise, if the parent tells you that during visitation time he or she doesn't allow the child to participate in extracurricular activities such as baseball games to avoid giving up any time with the child, that is also telling. A good parent understands that a child also has a life, with responsibilities within that life. A parent's job is to facilitate the child's success at fulfilling those responsibilities. Keeping the child away from a game because the parent doesn't want to give up time with the child is inappropriate. Also, ask whether Child Protective Services has ever been to the parent's home, and if so why. Ask about police visits as well. Ask whether the parent has ever been arrested, including when the arrest occurred and how it was resolved. Ask these questions of the stepparent as well if there is one. Finally, evaluate how determined this parent is to stay the course, no matter how hard, to be a significant part of the child's life. You will meet with parents whose goal is lowering their child support payments rather than being an active and consistent part of their child's life.

Phase 4

The fourth phase of the interview is talking specifically about each child. The court is only interested in children under the age of 18, but if there are children in the family older than 18, talk about them also. They are part of the family even if they aren't involved in this court proceeding. Ask the parent how old each child is; what grade he or she is in, and what school he or she attends. These seem like simple questions, but it is telling if the parent can't answer them. Ask the parent how the child does in school, what he or she enjoys most about school, and what he or she enjoys least. Discover whether the child has friends, both at school and out of school. Talk about any behavioral problems both in school and out of school. Find out what the child likes to do outside school. Inquire about the child's involvement in any extracurricular activities. If the child is young, ask about the child's developmental milestones, including potty training, bed-wetting, cosleeping, self-dressing, and personal hygiene chores, as well as prevalence of nightmares, nature of eating habits and bedtime rituals, and other such development-related matters. You are looking for red flags that may indicate that the child is suffering from the continuing conflict: the inconsistencies in life or other factors that are affecting the child's developmental progress. Discuss with the parent whether he or she has noticed any change in behaviors since the breakup of the family. Talk about the child's behaviors at the exchanges for visitation. Understand the nature of the transition the child goes through when changing from one home to another. Finally, ask the parent what he or she is most proud of about his or her child and what worries him or her the most about the child. Find out how much the parent knows about the child, and how in touch he or she is with the child. Find out how involved the parent is with the child, and discover what difficulties the child is currently experiencing.

Have the parent talk about the child in such a way as to help you understand the child's role in the family; this helps you get to know the child and how he or she might be struggling to cope with his or her family's breakup.

In a family with more than one child, after you have discussed each child separately, have the parent describe the family dynamics before and after the breakup. Have the parent discuss the role each child had in the original family and his or her new role in both of the two new families. Find out which of the children has taken on the adult role, which has checked out of the family's problems, which child is struggling with his or her emotions, and which is simply repressing his or her feelings. Ask how the children get along together. Find out which of the children is protecting which parent and which child holds the most anger toward which parent.

Most important, find out from both parents' perspectives how the children have changed since the breakup of their family. Every child changes as a result of a divorce. Some changes are easy to identify, but others are less so. As any child counselor knows, children don't significantly change their behavior without some reason. You need to know what changes have manifested, including when they began, how they have affected both the child's life and each parent's life, and to what each parent attributes these changes. It is telling whether the parent can answer these questions thoughtfully.

Phase 5

The fifth phase of the interview is discussing what the parent thinks would work best for the child when it comes to custody and visitation. You have listened to the parent tell you what is wrong with the other parent and why he or she believes the other parent should have limited time with the child. Now the parent gets the chance to tell you what he or she thinks would in fact work best with regard to custody and visitation. If he or she tells you that he or she wants to have the child during the school year with the other parent having alternate weekend visitation, that might make sense. If he or she goes on to tell you that the other parent can have weeks of uninterrupted summer visitation, that doesn't make sense. Didn't this parent just tell you that the other parent is incapable of taking care of the child? Now he or she has given the other parent more clock hours each day with the child then he or she has given himself or herself. These are the kinds of incongruencies that need to be addressed in the evaluation.

Sometimes parents think they have to give the other parent all summer if they have the child during the school year. This is not true. The family courts are not held to just a handful of visitation schedules. The court can order any type of visitation schedule that best meets the needs of the child. It may be true that courts often order alternate weekend visitation, but that doesn't mean always. One of the reasons the court orders an evaluation is that the court is interested in recommendations that use your professional creativity to suggest an appropriate visitation schedule.

Another paradigm shift that needs to be explained to both parents is the concept of clock time with the child. Often a parent wants the time during the school year and is willing to give the other parent the weekends and most of the summer. But it is clear that a child in school has two lives: One life is during the school week: The child sees his or her parent for a short time in the morning before school and for a few hours after school and then goes to bed. As a result, the actual clock hours with the parent during the school week are very limited. The child's other life is the weekends, holidays, and summer. During those times, the child has many potential clock hours to spend with the parent. So if a parent has the ability to spend those hours with his or her child, it would make sense to have the child on weekends and summer.

Let's assume that one of the parents is a school teacher and that the other works a traditional job. The teacher wants to have the child primarily during the school year and thinks the other parent should have alternate weekend visitation during the school year. Furthermore, the parent suggests that during the summer the other parent have the child during the week and the teacher have alternate weekend visitation. Assuming that both parents are equally qualified to parent the child, it makes little sense for the teacher to spend his or her summer days alone without the child and for the traditional working parent to spend his or her evenings after work and after school alone without the child. It is more sensible to have the child stay with the parent who is most available to the child in light of the parents' school and summer schedules. Thus, a recommended visitation schedule would be that the child would live primarily with the traditional working parent during the school year and visit on alternate weekends with the teacher. During the summer, the child would live primarily with the teacher and have alternate weekend visits with the traditional working parent. You might also recommend that each parent have some length of extended vacation time during the summer and also indicate a holiday schedule, such as dividing the Christmas holiday into the first and second week and alternating the weeks each year, splitting or alternating the spring break holiday and alternating the other holidays during the school year and the summer. This schedule actually gives both parents approximately equal time with the child—in other words, a shared arrangement.

During the fifth phase of the evaluation, you ask the parent for his or her input into what would work best for the child. It does not mean that you always agree with what the parent says, but it does mean that you get some idea of how the parents are thinking and why, including their motivations.

Listen carefully to what each parent thinks would work best for the child. Ask why the parent thinks his or hers is the best solution. The parent needs to be able to explain his or her thought process in coming up with the solution. Ask how the solution would benefit the child now and in the future. Finally, ask whether the parent has thought of any other ideas for visitation. If so, then ask why the parent decided against those other ideas. You can also make some suggestions for visitation. Be sure to tell the parent that these are only ideas, not necessarily reflective of what your recommendations will be to the court. Looking at other alternatives is a way to discern how flexible or rigid the parent is toward other, possibly more creative ideas for visitation. Some parents believe their idea is the only idea that could make sense. Other parents are willing to listen to other ideas and at least think about those ideas' pros and cons. You know that flexibility is a key component to effective coparenting. This is one way to assess a parent's flexibility and willingness to compromise.

Finally, ask each parent what he or she thinks the other parent will say about him or her during that parent's interview. This will give you insight into areas that need further discussion with the other parent and how in tune that parent is with the other parent's feelings.

Phase 6

The last phase is the summary and wrapup. Your job is to summarize what the parent has told you for the last couple hours. Tell the parent what you understand about his or her fears and concerns and about what he or she thinks would work for the child when it comes to custody and visitation; in addition, discuss the strengths and weaknesses of that parent's side of the case. This is not the time to tell the parent what you are thinking of recommending to the court, but rather the time to give closure to the parent's session with you.

Summary

The parent interview is an important time for you. Your counseling skills will serve you well in establishing a relationship in which the parent can talk openly with you. Let the conversation flow naturally. A series of questions doesn't work as well as a conversation to gather information. Most parents want an opportunity to tell their story: All they need is someone who is genuine, unbiased, and willing to hear. Many times the conversation moves from one time in their lives to another; your job is to follow along and come up with an accurate timeline. Often the conversation will not follow the six phases of an interview in order. That is fine so long as you come away with the information necessary to understand the parent and the parent's role in the child's life, hopes for the future, and ability to coparent and communicate with the other parent, as well as how the parent deals with conflict. Watch the time and don't run long. Move the parent along if he or she is going slowly, time is running out, and you haven't gotten all the information you need. Remember: This is your business, and time is money. It is your responsibility to make sure you get the information you need in the time allotted. As you become more practiced at conducting the interviews, you will better manage your time and get information without feeling rushed. Some evaluators do have the parents come for more than one session—you may choose to do so. However, a second session isn't the best use of your time if you can get what you need in one session.

Stepparent Interview

Stepparents or others who act in a stepparenting role must also be included in the evaluation. The evaluator needs to know all the adults who are participating in a parenting role in the child's life. If it is possible, schedule the parent's session when the stepparent can also attend. It is interesting to see how the two relate to each other and who seems to be running the show. The stepparent does not have a central role in the parent's session, but he or she does contribute to the session. Your job is to understand not only the stepparent's personhood but also his or her motivations, emotional stability, and strength of connection to the parent and the child. If the stepparent has children, talk about them as well. Find out how well adjusted the stepparent's children are, where they live, whether they have a visitation schedule with their other parent, and how they have accepted the new family these two adults have created for them. Understand how this family functions, when the children come and go for visitation, and how the adults incorporate the children into their lives.

Finally, you need to discover what the stepparent's philosophy is about being a stepparent. Does he or she put his or her own children and activities first? Is he or she a stepparent who has taken over the parenting job from the parent? Does he or she have a hands-off policy when it comes to the stepchild? Has he or she overstepped his or her appropriate boundaries with the child or distanced himself or herself from the child? Ideally, the child should like his or her stepparent, as it is better that the child be comfortable with the stepparent than not. However, it is not the stepparent's job to raise this child: The two parents of the child have the primary responsibility of raising and parenting the child together. Finally, you want to know what the stepparent's role is when it comes to the other parent. Do they know each other? Do they get along? Do they fight with each other? Does the stepparent start arguments between the two parents and then stand back and watch? Understand how the stepparent fits into the new family of this parent and the other family of the former spouse.

If the stepparent cannot come to the parent's appointment, then schedule a separate session with him or her, approximately 1 hour long. You have to get to know the stepparent from his or her own mouth. Often the stepparent is the assigned reason for the marriage's end. Whether or not that is true, the stepparent is going to have an influence on how the child is raised in one of the parent's homes and on how both of the child's parents are going to interact and ultimately raise their child.

After the sessions with both parents (and stepparents as applicable), you have a picture of the case. It is not complete, but it is beginning to take on color. Now is the time to interview the child.

CHILD INTERVIEW

You want to see for yourself how a parent interacts with his or her child. The parent has told you in his or her session with you what kind of relationship he or she has with the child. Now it is time to see how accurate the parent was in the telling. You need to schedule an appointment for the parent to bring the child to your office. The stepparent is not invited to this appointment. If he or she does come with the parent to the appointment, he or she must sit in the lobby during the appointment. If there is more than one child, the parent is scheduled to bring all the children together. This means all the children, regardless of age. You want to see how a parent deals with older children and an infant while completing the assigned task. You will tell the parent that he or she is going to do an activity with the child (or children) while you observe. After the activity, you will meet privately with each child involved in the case. You should also instruct the parent what to say to the child regarding this appointment. When the appointment is close, tell the parent to tell the child that everyone is going to see a person who is trying to help Mom and Dad get along better and who is going to try and make the child's life easier. Be sure to word the instructions appropriately for the age of each child. Tell the child that he or she is going to do an activity with the parent and then will spend a little time with you, the evaluator. Do not tell the parent to coach the child. Keep your instructions vague so that neither the parent nor child knows exactly what to expect from the appointment. Schedule at least 30 minutes for the activity and about 30 to 45 additional minutes per child (but less for younger children). Your goal is to observe the parent interacting with the child and to spend quality private time with the child.

Now you are beginning to understand why it is important that you have the skills necessary to work with children of all developmental levels. If you have the skills to work effectively with adolescents, focus on improving your skills working with preteens and younger children. If the child involved in the case is an infant, you won't have the parent do an activity with the child, but that doesn't mean that you don't want to meet the child and see the parent interact with the child. Remember, your voice is the child's voice in court, so you need to meet every child who is part of the case. If the child is an infant, schedule a 30-minute appointment for the parent to bring the child to your office. Schedule around naptime so the child is awake and active, allowing you to observe the parent's interactions with the child. Regardless of the age of the child, you need to be able to know whether the child is developing normally and mature or immature for his or her age, as well as how to interact and talk with the child. If you are weak in relating to children, then study, take classes or workshops, and enlist some aid through supervision to help you improve at relating to children.

Next, decide which activity you want the parent and child to do together. You should have a variety of activities to draw from that are appropriate to the age of the child. If you have access to a play therapy room, observe the parent interacting with the child in that room. This won't work if the child is older or if there are several children in the family. Some evaluators use a therapeutic sand tray for this activity. It works well with one child, but not if there are several children that you want to observe with the parent. It is not important what the activity is so long as it encourages interaction between the children, as well as the children and the parent. It also has to be big enough to occupy everyone for the allotted time.

One activity that works well with a variety of ages is collage building. You don't need much material for this activity, only magazines, large blank paper, colored markers or pencils, scissors, glue, and tape. Get a variety of magazines, including those about fashion, sports, outdoors, children's activities, gardening, and food. Get enough for the participants to have a good selection, but not so many that they feel overwhelmed. The blank paper on which they put their pictures should be large enough to hold quite a few pictures, but not so large that it can't be filled up. Many times children like to draw on a collage, so provide colored pencils, markers, and crayons. Provide both glue and tape—glue sticks work better than liquid glue. Finally, provide a selection of scissors for all ages. Provide more than two, but don't get one of everything for each participant. One thing you want to observe is how everyone shares with each other.

Parent/Child Activity

Tell everyone that you want them to build a collage. You may have to describe what a collage is; explain that everyone can make his or her own or everyone can work together and build one collage. The pictures they choose can be of things they like to do with their parent, things that interest them personally, or simply pictures they like. Then go and sit in the corner and observe the interactions the parent has with the child or children and how the child (or children) interacts with the parent. Also notice how the children interact with each other. Watch how compliant the children are with the parent's requests and whether the children are comfortable enough to give the parent instructions.

Other things you are observing are how engaged the children and the parent are in the task. Are the children working alone? Is the parent doing the work for them? Does the parent encourage the child effectively, or is praise ingenuous? Does the parent ignore some of the children and focus only on one child? Does the parent have the organizational skills necessary to complete the task? Do the children and parent seem happy to be doing something together? Is there one child who seems to be the boss of the other children, maybe even acting as a parent? Is there a child who appears to be helpless at gaining the parent's attention?

Other things to observe are the feelings in the room. Does there seem to be a sense of peace or of utter confusion and chaos? Do the children have a bad attitude toward the parent, possibly even being rude and disrespectful? Does the family use humor with each other, or do they pick on each other? Does the parent attend only to the younger children, ignoring the older children? Does the parent expect the older children to help the younger children? In other words, is there a sense of connection between the children and toward the parent? Do you get a sense of family among these people? Did the parent describe the child accurately during his or her appointment with you? Did the parent describe his or her relationship with the child well?

Give a 10-minute warning, then a 5-minute warning, then a 1-minute warning that the time is almost done. When the time is up, ask the children which one wants to talk to you first to tell you about the collage. Then excuse the parent and the other children to the lobby to wait their turn with you. Now you will spend time with each of the children apart from the parent.

Child's Private Session

Begin the session with the child by having him or her tell you about his or her collage. Let the child tell you why he or she picked the pictures he or she chose. If the parent did a separate collage, have the child tell you why he or she thinks the parent chose the pictures he or she chose. Then ask the child if he or she knows why he or she is talking with you. Older children will probably know why they are there. They will tell you that their parents fight and don't get along. Younger children may not know why they are there with you. Tell them that their parents do not know how to talk with each other well and that they often fight because of it. This will come as no surprise to the child: Remember that the child has been a part of the conflict between his or her parents from the beginning. Then tell the child that your job is to help their parents learn to get along better; explain that to do that, you are meeting with the child so that he or she can help you with that job.

Your next step is to tell the child what you already know about him or her. You can tell the child his or her age and grade in school and describe how well he or she does in school. Tell the child about his or her siblings, stepsiblings, and stepparent (if applicable). Talk to the child about his or her extracurricular activities. Then talk to the child about his or her relationships with the other people in his or her life.

Start with one of the parents and have the child talk about what he or she does with that parent, what that parent's house is like, whether the child has his or her own space in that house, whether the child feels safe in that house, and how the child gets along with the other children when at that parent's house. Talk to the child about what he or she likes best about being with that parent and what he or she likes least. Ask the child what he or she would change about being with that parent if it were possible. Then do the same for the other parent. Try to understand what the child's life is like when with each parent. Does the child spend time with the stepparent more than the parent? Does the child get along with the stepchildren, or is there fighting between them? Is the child treated the same as the other children when with that parent? Does the child spend quality time with the parent? Understand from the child's perspective what life is like now that the child has two families, two homes, and two different sets of rules to live by.

You also need to understand how the child feels when with either parent and how the child feels about the breakup of the family. Talk about how the child feels and thinks when the parents fight with each other or argue with the stepparent. Find out whether the child's emotional needs are being met by the parents. Ask about what worries the child and how he or she deals with those concerns. Find out, from the child's perspective, whether he or she is spending enough time with each parent. Don't ask the child what he or she wants for a visitation schedule, but do probe to find out whether the child's best interests are being met by the current schedule.

Depending on the age of the child, he or she will often tell you what the visitation schedule should be. Listen carefully to what the child thinks would work best. You don't have to agree, but you need to allow the child to have a voice in the schedule. Discover whether the child has a thoughtful reason for why his or her idea would work better than what is happening now. For example, if the child tells you that he wants to spend half his or her time with Mom and half with Dad because Dad is sad when he or she isn't there, that may well mean that the child has taken on the role of Dad's protector. But this isn't a role any child should have to bear: Dad's happiness is, of course, Dad's business. If Mom wants to move to another state and the child wants to move also because "there are fireflies and cardinals there," the child's reasoning is probably reflecting Mom's attempts to talk the child into wanting to move. Always listen to hear whether the child's thoughts are his or her own.

Occasionally the child will not want to talk about the parents at all, giving brief answers or no answers at all. The child will change the subject and talk about other things, or maybe even tell you that he or she doesn't want to talk about life with either parent. This is telling to an evaluator. Generally this means that it is too painful to talk about how the child lives and feels when with either parent. It may also mean that the child doesn't want to say the wrong thing and get either parent "in trouble." The child's silence is revealing of his or her adjustment to life after the breakup of the family. If this happens and the child refuses to talk about the parents, just let it go. It is not your job to be the child's therapist, nor to make the child feel uncomfortable spending time with you. Talk about what the child wants to talk about, and leave things at that.

Always leave the session with the child on a positive note. Tell the child that you understand how different his or her life is now and how hard things can be sometimes. Find out what the child does well and encourage him or her to continue to do it well. Encourage the child to continue to do well in school so that he or she will have choices and opportunities in the future. Talk with the child about how his or her new life will get better with time. Don't tell the child that his or her parents will get along and quit fighting, but rather that even if the parents continue to fight and not get along with each other, even that will get better as time passes. Help the child understand that it is not his or her job to keep either parent happy or protect him or her—that is the parent's job. Leave the child feeling some hope, but don't lie: You don't know what order will come from the court, so don't make promises to the child about how the case will work out. Let the child know that however the case ends, he or she will still be able to make his or her own choices and have the opportunity to direct his or her own life toward the best future possible.

Now you understand why it is so important to develop relationships quickly and know the developmental needs of children of different ages. You always get information about the child even if he or she is hesitant to talk with you. You find out whether the child is developing appropriately, whether the child spends a lot of time thinking about his or her parents, whether the child is angry at one parent, who the child blames for the breakup of the family, which parent better meets the child's needs, and how the child wishes his or her life could be different. You also find out how mature the child is or how needy he or she is for positive emotional attachment with the parents. Through this information, you can determine the child's primary caregiver. You can also determine whether one parent seems to have more influence over the child than the other.

Notes

After you have seen all the children, write your notes about your time with each child. Do this immediately after the session so that your thoughts are fresh. Since you don't take notes when you are talking to the child, writing your notes soon after the session is important to maintaining accuracy. In your notes, mention how developmentally appropriate each child is, and how mature or immature the child is for his or her age. Note whether the child engaged in conversation with you or avoided talking about the parents. Note how the child feels about all the people in his or her life and how well the child gets along with them—or doesn't. If the child said how he or she would like life to be different, write that down. If the child had an idea about a visitation schedule, note that. Your notes should also reflect the emotional health of the child, what role he or she has assumed, and how well he or she seems to be handling life with two families. If the child seemed to be overly coached by a parent, mention that in your notes and explain why you reached that conclusion. Finally, note which parent is the child's primary caregiver.

After you write about each child separately, write in your notes about the similarities between the children. Did the children all talk about how their parents' fighting upsets them? Did they all mention that their stepparent was unfair to them? Did they all talk about getting along all right with their stepparent and stepsiblings? Remember: Your notes need to be thorough enough to remind you of your time with the child and any conclusions you made after talking to the child. Finally, if you noticed things that need to be dealt with by the parents to make the child's life easier or better, note those. Perhaps the child would benefit from counseling, being involved in extracurricular activities, or being tested in school for possible learning disability, speech therapy, tutoring, or other services.

Now you will have seen the parents, seen the parents interacting with their child, and spoken to the child privately. It is time to make collateral contacts.

COLLATERAL CONTACTS

Ask both parents for some collateral contacts with whom they would like you to get in touch. You won't necessarily contact them all, but you need names and numbers for when you do. If a parent asks whose names the other parent provided, answer honestly. Remember: There are no secrets in a custody evaluation. Always ask for copies of report cards for all the children. If there is evidence that a child's grades have changed since the divorce or since a change in visitation, ask for prior report cards to verify this. Be sure the report cards show the number of absences and tardies. You may have to verify which parent had the child when the absences and tardies occurred. You will always contact the child's counselor (if he or she has a current or recent one), the parent's counselor, and the daycare provider for children who are not in school. If there is a difference in opinion between the parents about how the child is doing in school, or if there are questions about the report card, then contact the teacher.

The Child's Counselor

Tell the parent to sign a release of information with the counselor. The counselor keeps the release in his or her files. Because you are working under a court order, you probably don't need the release, but getting it makes things easier and more understandable for the counselor. Tell the parent what you are going to ask the counselor when you speak to him or her: how long the counselor has seen the parent or child and how often (weekly or biweekly), what the presenting problem was, what the treatment plan is, what progress is being made in counseling, what difficulties have arisen in the counseling process, and what the counselor's thoughts are about the child. During the contact, inquire whether the counselor has an opinion about the parents' parenting skills, how well the parent copes with stress and conflict, what the parent needs to do to make his or her and the child's life more positive, and whether the counselor has an opinion about custody and a visitation schedule.

While you are talking to the counselor, ask whether he or she has observed the parent with the child. Determine whether the counselor has met both parents and find out his or her thoughts and impressions about both. Get the counselor's overall impression of the child and what he or she predicts for the child's future positive growth as well as any looming problems for the child.

Be sure to inquire about the counselor's thoughts regarding the child's feelings toward the divorce, the current visitation schedule, the stepparents, and the stepsiblings. Discuss with the counselor who he or she believes is the child's primary caregiver and why. Solicit the counselor's opinion of the current custody and visitation schedule and how workable it is for the child.

The child's counselor knows the child better than you do simply by virtue of having spent more time with the child. Therefore, he or she is a good resource with whom to check out your initial opinions about the child and the parents. Be sure to take good notes as you are talking. Again, if you don't know the counselor, ask about his or her education, licensure, and training to work with children. Also find out how long he or she has been in practice counseling with children.

The Parent's Counselor

If one of the parents is engaged in counseling currently or has been in counseling in the recent past, it is reasonable to contact his or her counselor. Have the parent sign a release of information with his or her counselor. When you talk to the counselor, ask how long he or she has seen the parent, how often he or she schedules sessions, what the presenting problem was, what the treatment plan is, and how much progress has been made toward termination.

Discuss the client's parenting skills, what is enhancing those skills, and what is detrimental to the parent's being a successful parent. Inquire whether the counselor has observed the parent and child together. Ask him or her to comment on potential pitfalls for the parent in the future to describe the strengths the parent can use to deal with those stressors. Ask whether the counselor has any opinion about the current custody and visitation schedule and whether he or she has any concerns about the ability of his or her client to parent at least adequately.

Of course, if you don't know the counselor, ask for information regarding his or her degree, licensure, and time in practice. Be sure to take notes while you are talking to the counselor to revisit later as you consider your recommendations for this case.

The Teacher or Child Care Provider

Sometimes evaluators talk to the child's teacher; however, if the report cards reflect what both parents tell you, then it probably isn't necessary. Remember: Each case stands on its own merits, so you may choose to speak to the teacher, but likely you will not. If the child is seeing the school counselor, of course you will talk to him or her. Have the parent sign a release of information with the school or the school counselor. If the child is not in school, contacting the child care provider is a reasonable thing to do if he or she is not a relative of either parent.

The child care provider can tell you about the child's developmental progress and behaviors. He or she can also tell you how often the child misses daycare and whether the child comes fed, cleaned, and with appropriate equipment, as well as arguments the parents have had at the daycare, whether the bill is being paid, how receptive the parents are to feedback from the child care provider, and the emotional stability of the child. The child care provider may well have an opinion about who the primary caregiver is for the child and what kind of custody and visitation schedule would work best for the child. Be sure to take good notes while you are talking to the child care provider. Also, ask him or her how long he or she has been a provider, whether the facility is licensed, how many children the provider is responsible for, and the details of the provider's education and training.

Documentation

The last of the collateral material is the documentation provided to you either by the attorney or by the parent. Knowing what documentation you need is tricky. You don't want to be overwhelmed by paperwork, but neither do you want to miss some documents that will help you make appropriate recommendations. However, generally less paper is better.

Many times the parent will ask you what paperwork he or she should bring to his or her appointment with you. You may want specific documents for some particular reason, so tell the parent to bring copies of those documents for you to keep. Generally, though, you won't know what, if any, documents you will need. Tell the parent he or she is welcome to bring copies of what might help you better understand the parent's perspective on the case. Most people bring nothing with them, and that is usually fine. During the interview, if there are specific documents you need, you can tell the parent to make copies of those documents and bring them to his or her appointment with the child. If the parent brings and leaves something with you, however, you must read it.

Types of documentation that may be helpful are arrest records, original divorce order with custody and visitation schedule detailed, modification paperwork, and other evaluations, which may be previous custody evaluations, psychological evaluations, and previous mediation agreements. Through the interview with both parents you will have already gained this information. Therefore, the question is whether these documents can give you more information than you already have. If so, then get copies. If not, then save your time and don't request them. You already have the court order for the custody evaluation with your instructions included, as well as information about what the original custody and visitation schedule were and whatever changes have occurred over time. You already know what each parent wants and who filed the modification and what the modification is requesting. So don't spend your time rereading these documents unless they will provide you with new and useful information.

Occasionally, the attorney will provide you with documentation that he or she believes will assist you in the evaluation. Sometimes it will; sometimes not. Regardless, if you get these documents, you are responsible for reading them. Overlooking documentation provided to you by either the parent or the attorney is not acceptable. If you possess it, you must read it and consider it.

Home Visits

Occasionally, you will be asked to conduct a home visit in both parents' homes. You are going to have to decide before beginning what you are going to do in response to such a request. Most evaluators do not do home visits. If the parents have vastly different perspectives about the other's living space and arrangements, the evaluator can request that Child Protective Services, through the appropriate department of health and welfare, conduct the home visit. Most evaluators do not see home visits as part of their job description. But if you do decide to do home visits, be sure you will be safe doing the visit and will glean helpful information from the visit. Unexpected visits probably give better and more accurate information about the parent's living situation, but taking your time to drive to the home in hopes that the parent is there and that he or she will let you in is a gamble. Alternatively, setting up an in-home visit ahead of time will probably give you an unrealistic look at the parent and the home. Spending hours at the home may give you insight into the parent's parenting style but is a poor use of your time and is hardly cost-effective. You will be able to gain the same information about the parent through your interviews. So make up your mind whether you are going to do home visits or let others do them if they become necessary. Generally speaking, home visits are not necessary or helpful, and they certainly are not cost-effective for you.

Other Considerations

There may be other collateral contacts you want to talk to as part of the evaluation. However, talking to relatives of the parents is usually a bad idea. Not only does it put the relative in a bad position if he or she tells you something bad about the parent, but generally he or she will only tell you wonderful things about his or her son or daughter and horrible things about the other parent. It makes sense that the parent will align himself or herself with his or her relation. If you already know what a person is going to tell you, then there is generally no good reason for contacting him or her.

Making collateral contacts is time-consuming and thus money-consuming. Make a rule about how many times you will try to contact a collateral contact. Make a concerted effort to talk to each one by leaving messages explaining why you are calling and when and how you can be reached. Remember: Many counselors working with children have office hours in the evening, so they may have to call you after your office closes and even in the evening. Be sure to keep an accurate record of the date, time, and contents of each message you left each time you try to get in touch with a contact. If you ultimately can't make contact with a particular person, note that down.

Now you have completed your interviews with the parents, the stepparents, the child and parent together, and the child alone. You have made collateral contacts and gathered whatever documentation is helpful. You are now ready to write your report to the court.

Writing the Report

GENERAL GUIDELINES

You have collected all the information you need to write your report to the court. You have a complete picture of this family—how it was before the breakup and how it is functioning now. You have identified the child's primary caregiver. You understand which parent can offer the child the most consistency and stability in life. You have discovered how the child's new family systems work. You also understand the issues between the parents and between the child and his or her parents. You have identified how the child fits into these new systems and what issues they cause the child. And you have a professional opinion about what best serves the child's interest. You are ready to suggest a custody and visitation schedule, and you have reasons backing up your suggestion.

Before you begin writing the report, take time to think about the case. Allow the facts and issues of the case to percolate in your mind. Writing the report before allowing yourself the opportunity to really contemplate the intricacies of this case is premature. Think before you write. You don't need to think for weeks, but take at least some time, a day or two or even three. Have the report at least outlined in your head before you sit down to write it.

When writing the report, remember that less is more. The more you write, the more ammunition you give the attorney arguing against your report. You have reasons for all your opinions, but you don't want to set yourself up for a difficult time testifying in court. You must write a report that is complete and understandable by the attorneys, the court, and the parents. However, the report does not have to include every nuance behind your decisions. It will include some information, but need not include all your thought processes in reaching your conclusions. Some evaluators write lengthy, wordy reports. You may choose to write reports this way, but remember that what everyone really wants to read is the recommendations. When the attorneys and judges get your report, they will inevitably turn first to the page headed Recommendations.

You are the child's voice in court. Your recommendations are written to ensure that the child's best interests are protected while he or she maintains appropriate contact with his or her parents. Every family court in each jurisdiction has the child's best interests as the primary focus. Although laws vary in wording between states, the commonalities between jurisdictions are striking. Generally speaking, family courts look at all relevant factors promoting the child's best interests, including the wishes of the child's parent or parents; the wishes of the child; the interaction and inter-relationship of the child with his or her parents and siblings; the child's adjustment to his or her home, school, and community; the mental and physical health and integrity of all adults involved with the child; the need to promote stability and continuity in the child's life; and the existence, if any, of domestic violence in the presence of the child. In other words, what best promotes the child's positive emotional, physical, and developmental growth? Now you understand even better why the job of an evaluator is not for the faint of heart. First, you are working with parents who do not, cannot, and will not get along with each other. You are facing attorneys whose job is to advocate for their client regardless of, even in spite of, his or her parenting abilities. Last, you are working for the child and writing recommendations to serve his or her best interests. This generally means that both the parents are going to be angry about your recommendations. Neither parent is going to get everything he or she requested during his or her time with you, nor is he or she going to feel very happy toward you and your work. Nevertheless, you must make your recommendations.

TRANSMITTAL LETTER

Write the report on your letterhead, which includes your name, the full name of your license, your license number, your address, and your telephone number:

Jane Doe, PhD, LPC, NCC 100 BOULEVARD ROAD #201
ALABAMA LICENSED PROFESSIONAL COUNSELOR #100 GREAT
  CITY, AL 83250
NATIONAL CERTIFIED COUNSELOR #100 208-208-9999

On your letterhead, write a letter to the judge to transmit your report. It is copied to both attorneys. The letter is short, stating what is enclosed and giving your contact information in case of any questions:

January 1, 2014

JUDGE ROBERT PETERSON
SIXTH DISTRICT MAGISTRATE COURT
CENTRAL COUNTY COURT HOUSE
GREAT CITY, AL 83250
RE: SMITH VS SMITH
CASE NO.: CV-0021-DR
Dear Judge Peterson:
    Enclosed please find my recommendations regarding custody and visitation of the Smith children.
    Please contact me with any additional questions.

Sincerely,
Jane Doe, PhD, LPC, NCC

cc: Attorney #1
        Attorney #2

THE ACTUAL REPORT

Data Summary

The first page of the report begins on letterhead. The report begins with a summary of the data gathering procedures. This could be a list of the dates of the appointments and the participants of the appointments. Generally, the length of time of the appointment is not included. Next is a list of the information sources (collateral contacts) and any documentation used by the evaluator in reaching his or her conclusions:

RECOMMENDATIONS OF CUSTODY AND VISITATION
OF THE SMITH CHILDREN

RE: SMITH VS SMITH

CASE NO.: CV-0021-DR

DATE: JAN. 1, 2014

SUMMARY OF DATA GATHERING PROCEDURES:

DATES OF SERVICE
11-14-2013   BOB SMITH (NO-SHOW—RESCHEDULE)
11-18-12   BOB SMITH and HEATHER ADAMS
11-20-12   JANE SMITH
11-23-12   BOB and CHILDREN
11-23-12   CHILDREN
11-30-12   JANE and CHILDREN
11-30-12   CHILDREN

COLLATERAL CONTACTS
12-02-12   CHILDREN'S COUNSELOR—SUSAN JONES
12-10-12   JANE'S COUNSELOR—ROBERT JONES
12-12-12   CHILD CARE PROVIDER—AMY

DOCUMENTATION USED
REPORT CARDS OF SUZY, JOHN, AND KATHY
ORIGINAL DIVORCE ORDER
MODIFICATION REQUEST—BOB SMITH
MODIFICATION REQUEST—JANE SMITH
ARREST RECORD—BOB

PAYMENTS
11-18-12   BOB $1000.00
11-20-12   JANE $1000.00
PAID IN FULL

You also might include the heading Assessments, under which you provide the name of any assessment as well as when it was administered and who conducted it. If there were other types of data collection, include those under the appropriate headings.

Interview Summaries

After you have provided all the appropriate data, summarize the interviews, collateral contacts, and assessments (if given). Remember that less is more when it comes to the summaries: It is reasonable to highlight the concerns and positives of the interviews, but do not overelaborate on any point.

SUMMARY OF SUZY SMITH INTERVIEW

Suzy Smith, age 14, was interviewed privately on November 23, 2012, and November 30, 2012. Suzy is in the 8th grade at Jefferson Junior High School, located in Great City, Alabama. Suzy's recent report card indicates that she is an excellent student. She has all As and Bs on her report card. She has not been excessively tardy, nor has she missed many days of school.

Suzy easily engaged in the task with both her mother and her father. She interacted with both her parents appropriately. She was compliant with both parents' requests and was not hesitant to give either parent instructions during the task. Suzy also related well with her siblings. She shared equipment with them and offered assistance when asked.

Suzy was developmentally appropriate for her age. She was well groomed and appeared healthy. She was adultlike in many of her interactions with both her siblings and her parents. During the private interview, she acknowledged that she resented having to care for her siblings and stated that she bore a lot of the responsibility for caring for her younger siblings at both her mother's home and her father's home. There were times when she resented having to be her siblings' "mother." She did feel she had the ability to care for her siblings.

Suzy talked about the conflict between her mother and her father. She thinks that things got worse between them after her father's girlfriend moved into his house. Suzy likes Heather, but she wishes Heather would not take so much of her father's time. She said that Heather did not hit her or treat her badly. She also reported that Heather did not treat the other children badly, either. She believes that Heather makes her father happy, although Heather and her father do have arguments. She has never seen either Heather or her father hit each other.

Suzy feels safe and comfortable in both of her parents' homes. She has her own bedroom in each home and has her personal items at each home. She worries about her father when she is not with him because he seems so sad. She is glad that Heather is with her father when they aren't there. She also worries about her mother because she seems so alone. Suzy tries to spend as much time as possible with her mother in an attempt to make her happy.

Suzy hates it when her parents talk badly about each other and hates it when they fight in front of the children. She told about when her mother called the police to her father's home out of fear that they were left there alone. She felt embarrassed and angry when the police showed up, because she was left to care for the other children and considers herself capable of doing so. She was angry that her mother didn't think she could take care of her siblings and was angry at her father for taking Heather out to dinner instead of staying home with her and her siblings.

Suzy volunteered that the current visitation schedule meets her needs; she wants it to remain the same. She would be willing to change and spend more time at her father's home if there were a guarantee that her father would spend the extra time with her and the other children. She is looking forward to graduating from high school so that she can go to college and get away from all the drama.

It is apparent that Suzy loves both her parents and that she wants to spend time with both of them. She has a workable relationship with Heather. She wants her parents to stop fighting with each other and try to get along. She is a thoughtful child and mature for her age.

This summary tells the basics of what happened during the two interviews but does not go into the intricate details. What you write here must be reflected in your recommendations for custody and visitation. Be sure everything you write has a reason behind it and that everything ties together. For example, you can't write that the child is well adjusted and then recommend that he or she be evaluated for severe psychological problems.

ASSESSMENT SUMMARY

After summarizing the interviews, summarize the assessment results, if any. Be sure to note not just a diagnosis, but also what this diagnosis means for the parent's ability to parent effectively. It does no good to suggest that the parent struggles with depression based on the results of the assessment. What you need to explain is that although the parent may struggle with depression, the depression is not so debilitating that he or she can't be employed (the parent holds a full-time job) and deal with the children's academic responsibilities (the parent is a room parent, attends all parent–teacher conferences, transports the children to and from school, and so forth) or is unable to parent the children.

Remember not to rely solely on assessment results when developing your recommendations. In fact, your clinical skills will reap the most—and best—information about all the people involved in a case. Use the assessment results as confirmation of your judgments and observations. Do not use the results of an assessment as better information than the information you gleaned from your time spent with these people. You and your clinical skills—listening to these people, hearing what they say and don't say—will tell you far more than an assessment will. The assessment may give additional data, but it will not give you the rich information that you will obtain through talking with and listening to each person.

RECOMMENDATIONS—CUSTODY AND VISITATION

Your recommendations are what everyone is interested in. They speak to the child's best interest now and in the future. Remember: Your recommendations are based on your reasoned professional judgment and studied thought. They are not written to make one parent happy or to make one attorney happy, but rather to help the child progress positively in his or her life. The recommendations are also based in the reality of the case. It may well be that neither parent is particularly outstanding in his or her parenting skills, but these are the child's parents nonetheless—that is the child's reality—so your recommendations give the child his or her best shot at a positive future with the parents he or she has.

Before you write your recommendations, reflect on the picture you have of the parents, the children, the family that was, and the family that currently remains. Reflect on the developmental needs of the child. Think about what the child is struggling with and how your recommendations might lessen that struggle. Understand clearly what you are going to recommend and why, then start writing.

Recommendations generally begin with custody. The custody recommendation will reflect whether the parents should have joint custody or one parent have sole custody. Remember: Sole custody generally means that one parent is so incapacitated as a parent as to cause harm to the child by having responsibility for making decisions with the other parent for the child. If in your professional judgment you believe the child would be in danger from one parent, then recommend sole custody. Be prepared, however, to clearly explain your rationale during court testimony.

The second recommendation deals with visitation: which parent the child will generally live with while visiting regularly with the other parent. If you recommend supervised visitation, be sure you can explain why. You also must provide a suitable supervisor in such a case (it is generally not acceptable for the parents to find their own supervisor). Then delineate the structure of the recommended visitation schedule.

Included in the details of the visitation schedule are exchange times and places, days of visitation, sharing of travel costs, and (if necessary) how long a parent should wait for the other parent to appear for the exchange and how many times each parent should try to contact the other parent before leaving the exchange place. Additionally, the recommendation will include a holiday schedule, a summer schedule, a child–parent phone contact schedule, and what should be sent and brought back with the child (e.g., winter clothes, sports equipment). The right of first refusal for child care may also be recommended in this section. Each case is different and stands on its own merits, so sometimes the recommendation schedule is very detailed and complex, and sometimes it is a general guideline for the parents, who can then negotiate the exact terms.

RECOMMENDATIONS OF CUSTODY AND VISITATION OF THE JONES CHILDREN

RE: JONES VS JONES

CASE NO.: CV-000-00-DR

DATE: JANUARY 12, 2014

1. Joint custody of Sam Jones and Ben Jones be awarded to both parents, Mary Jones and Joe Jones.
2. It is recommended that the children live mostly with their mother, Mary, while visiting regularly with their father, Joe:
   a) Joe Jones would have visitation with the boys on alternate weekends from Friday evening to Sunday evening. Generally, all long weekends during the school year (e.g., 3-day weekends, teacher in-service) would be awarded to Joe. On a 3-day weekend, Joe's visitation would be Friday evening to Monday evening. Additionally, Joe would have an evening visit each week. Currently, the boys swim on Tuesday, and Joe coaches the swim team, so Joe's midweek visit would be Tuesday from after school to 8 p.m.
   b) Summer visitation for Joe would include 1 week (7 consecutive overnights) in each of the months of June, July, and August. The week visit would include one of the alternate weekends that Joe has visitation. It is Joe's responsibility to inform Mary which week he will have for visitation at least 4 weeks prior to the weeklong visitation. It is assumed that Joe will be available for child care during the extended vacation time.
   c) Holidays would generally be split or alternated as negotiated by the parents. Spring break would generally be awarded to Joe.

d) Regular phone contact between the children and their parents needs to be established. The parents can negotiate the time each day for the phone contact or they can allow the children to initiate the calls. It is both parents' responsibility to facilitate the daily phone contact.

e) Travel between City 1 and City 2 would be shared equally by the parents.

Here's another example:

RECOMMENDATIONS OF CUSTODY AND VISITATION OF THE MING CHILDREN

RE: MING VS MING

CASE NO.: CV-000-000-DR

DATE: MARCH 21, 2014

1. Joint custody of Mindy, Hong, Daniel, Robert, and Mong be awarded to both parents, Chan Ming and Chinn Ming.

2. It is recommended that the children live mostly with their mother, Chinn Ming, while visiting regularly with their father, Chan Ming:

   a) Chan would have alternate weekend visitation with the children from Friday evening to Sunday evening. The parents can negotiate the exchange times. Extended weekends would generally be awarded to Chan (e.g., 3-day weekends, teacher in-service) if he is available to provide child care for the children. Extended weekend visitation would be, for example, Friday evening to Monday evening on a 3-day weekend. Additionally, on the nonweekend visitation week Chan would have one evening visit. The parents can negotiate the day and times for the evening visitation.

   b) Summer visitation would include alternate weekend visitation from Friday evening to Monday morning. Additionally, Chan would have a 2-week extended vacation time twice during the summer (total of 4 nonconsecutive weeks). It is his responsibility to inform Chinn at least 4 weeks prior to the extended time when he will be using the extended summer visitations. It is assumed that Chan will be available to provide child care during the extended visitation times.

   c) Holidays can be split or alternated as negotiated by the parents. Christmas holiday can be split and the weeks alternated between the parents. Spring break would generally be awarded to Chan if he is available to care for the children.

   d) Regular phone contact between the children and their parents needs to be established. The parents can negotiate the time each day that the children will have phone contact with the other parent. The children can initiate the call, but it is the responsibility of both parents to facilitate the daily calls.

e) Both parents have the right of first refusal for child care. Additionally, both parents need to agree on any child care providers for the children.

Here's an example of visitation for 3 weekends each month:

RECOMMENDATIONS OF CUSTODY AND VISITATION OF ROBERTO HERNANDEZ

RE: HERNANDEZ VS HERNANDEZ

CASE NO.: CV-0000-0000-DR

DATE: JULY 12, 2014

1. Joint custody of Roberto Hernandez remains with both his parents, Maria Hernandez and Juan Hernandez.
2. It is recommended that Roberto continue to live mostly with his mother, Maria Hernandez, while visiting regularly with his father, Juan Hernandez:
   a) Juan will have visitation 3 weekends each month from Thursday evening (when he gets home from work) to Sunday evening. The parents can negotiate the actual exchange times. On the week without a weekend visitation, Juan will have a midweek visit from when he gets off work until 7 p.m. The parents can negotiate the day for the midweek visit.
   b) Summer visitation would remain the same with the addition of extended vacation time of 4 additional overnights (7 consecutive overnights) for each of June, July, and August. It is the responsibility of whichever parent is using the extended time to inform the other parent at least 3 weeks prior to using the extended time.
   c) Holidays can be split or alternated as negotiated by the parents. Spring break would generally be awarded to Juan. Christmas vacation could be split and the weeks alternated each year.
   d) Regular phone contact between Roberto and his parents needs to be established. The parents can negotiate the time for this daily phone contact. It is the responsibility for both parents to facilitate this phone contact.
   e) Both parents need to agree on who can drive for the exchanges. Ideally it would be the parents that do the exchanges, but some circumstances require that other people need to drive for the exchanges.
   f) Both parents have the right of first refusal for child care.

Finally, here's an example of a shared arrangement:

RECOMMENDATIONS OF CUSTODY AND VISITATION
OF THE WOODS CHILDREN

RE: COOPER VS WOODS

CASE NO.: CV-0000-0000-DR

DATE: OCTOBER 23, 2014

1. Joint custody of Amy Woods, Jenny Woods, and Alex Woods remains with both parents, Susan Cooper and Jason Woods.

2. Currently, the parents have a week/week shared arrangement. There are no compelling reasons at this time to change the week/week shared arrangement. Some modifications of the shared arrangements are recommended, however, in an effort to facilitate the parents' coparenting effectiveness:

   a) The parents will establish a time each week to communicate with each other regarding the children and their activities. This communication will be either face-to-face or on the phone. Effective communication does not happen through texting or e-mailing. During these weekly communication opportunities, the parents will establish who is responsible that week for taking the children to their extracurricular activities, appointments, game schedules, and so forth. If the parent responsible for transportation cannot fulfill that responsibility, he or she will contact the other parent first before making arrangements for someone else to drive the children. Furthermore, the parents will discuss medical concerns about the children, any bills that are outstanding, and any other topics related to the children.

   b) Both Jenny and Alex do not have school on Friday. Therefore, the children will spend Fridays with their mother, Susan, until 5 p.m.

   c) Both parents will be actively involved in Alex's medical care. Both parents must be diligent about requiring Alex to take his medicine before eating, watching his weight gain/loss, and facilitating his exercise and daily chest treatments. Both parents should attend his doctor appointments. Both parents also need to keep the other informed about the amount of time he exercises, what he is eating, and so on. Alex's chronic condition needs the careful attention of both parents. This attention is not enhanced when the parents are more interested in pointing out the other's flaws in Alex's treatment than in talking with each other to verify that everything that should be done for his well-being is being done.

   d) It is reasonable for either parent to request an evening visit with the children during the other parent's week. It is expected that both parents will facilitate the other's relationship with the children. The parents can either negotiate an evening visit or remain flexible and allow the evening visits to happen upon request.

   e) Both parents need to regularly give each of the children quality one-on-one time. In light of the number of stepsiblings in Jason's home, it is important that Jason's children have quality time to enhance their relationships with their father. Quality time is also a must between Susan and the children.

f) Regular phone contact between the children and their parents needs to be better facilitated by both parents. The parents can negotiate the time for this daily phone contact or can allow the children to initiate the calls each day.

g) Both parents have the right of first refusal for child care. Both parents need to respect this right for the other parent and contact the other parent when the children need care.

h) Both parents have the responsibility to agree upon any child care providers, other than each other, for the children. Susan does not want Bob (the 15-year-old stepson) to be responsible for the children, so he will not be providing child care in the future. It is also important that Amy not be used continually as a child care provider for her siblings or stepsiblings.

All these examples have some similarities. Joint custody is recommended in all four cases. Both parents have access to the children without supervision. In some cases, the children live mostly with their mother while visiting regularly with their father. This does not mean that there will not be some cases when the children live mostly with their father while visiting regularly with their mother. One of the examples recommends a shared arrangement between the parents. The visitation schedules are different, sometimes recommending alternate weekends and evening visits, sometimes 3 weekend visits. Summer visitation schedules vary depending on the case and the availability of the parents to provide child care. The holiday schedules are more detailed in some of the cases and left up to the parent's negotiations in others. All the examples recommend the right of first refusal for child care—some cases will not include this recommendation. Regardless, all the recommendations reflect the intricacies of each individual case such a way as to provide the attorneys and the court with your professional opinion in this case. The recommendations speak to the child's best interests now and in the future, based on your reasoned professional judgment and thought.

RECOMMENDATIONS—OTHER CONSIDERATIONS

Now let's look at recommendations that will facilitate the child's best interests in other ways besides custody and visitation. These recommendations range from counseling for the child and the parents to divorce education classes for the parents and extracurricular activities for the child. Be sure to include possible referrals for parent counselors, child counselors, and any classes. The parents, attorneys, and the court will not know the appropriate referrals, so you must provide them in your report. Of course, this means that you need to stay abreast of potential service providers in the area and have knowledge of their skills and expertise. The report you write has to delineate the custody and visitation schedule that will be best for the child, but it also has to point out the good qualities of both parents' skills. If a parent is not able to care for the child or is a danger to the child, you must include that in your recommendations. However, most of the reports you write will recommend that both parents have some type of access to the child. Your report will further expand on the good qualities of the parents and child and enhance them by providing referrals for services to both such as counseling or other activities.

Your report will also provide recommendations for improving the coparenting skills of the parents by recommending communication opportunities between the parents about their child. Depending on the case, this communication opportunity may be face-to-face or over the phone. For other cases, the communication may need to begin with e-mails and then move to the phone. Recommending texting to each other as a means of communication is probably better than nothing, but not by much. Texting does not improve communication between people, and it certainly doesn't provide for effective and appropriate coparenting.

Here are some examples of these types of recommendations from different cases not previously mentioned:

3. Both parents would benefit from parent education/divorce education classes. Possible referrals for the classes can be obtained from the Department of Children and Family Services.
4. All the children, especially Suzy and Bobby, would benefit from counseling services. Bobby is currently in counseling. Suzy would also benefit from individual counseling. Jeff and Sherry would benefit from being members of a divorce therapy group. The school counselor may provide this service at the school for the students at no cost. Mike would benefit from child therapy with a counselor skilled in play therapy. Possible referrals can also be obtained from the Department of Children and Family Services using its counselor referral list. This list contains appropriate counselors in the family's geographic area.
5. All the children are involved in extracurricular activities. Both parents need to support and encourage the children in these activities. The costs of the extracurricular activities will be shared equally between the parents.
6. Jane (the mother) is currently in counseling and should remain in regular counseling. Additionally, Jane would benefit from the services provided

by the Center for New Directions. The CND provides career counseling services at no cost. The CND is located on the College of USA campus. Jane needs to become financially independent as soon as possible.

7. Eric (the father) has recently found full-time employment. He needs to remain employed full-time to provide financial security for himself and his children. He also needs to find adequate housing for himself and the children.

8. Eric would also benefit from counseling services provided by a licensed therapist. Counseling would provide him the opportunity to improve his parenting, communication, and coparenting skills.

9. A regular time each week needs to be established for the parents to communicate with each other about the children. The parents can negotiate the day and time for this weekly communication opportunity.

10. A formal reevaluation may be necessary as the children age and their needs and best interests change. It is hoped that if there is a need to modify the custody and visitation schedule, both parents will have become successful coparents and can communicate with each other effectively and can modify the schedule without a formal reevaluation. If a formal reevaluation is necessary, it should consider the coparenting abilities of both parents, their effective communication skills with each other and the children, and the children's ages and developmental levels. Depending on relevant circumstances, the reevaluation should consider whether the current custody and visitation or a shared arrangement would better meet the children's best interests.

_____

Evaluator's name, degree, license, certifications   DATE

Here is another different example not previously mentioned:

3. Both children would benefit from individual counseling to help them better understand their feelings and their roles as children of a divorced family. Possible referrals include Dr. Smith (Good City), ABC Counseling Center (Good City), or Ms. Watson at XYZ Counseling Center (Falls City).

4. Both parents would also benefit from parent education/divorce education classes. Possible referrals include the ABC Counseling Center, XYZ Counseling Center, or MNO Counseling Center. Both parents would also benefit from individual counseling to help them better understand their emotions and their felt need for revenge on the other parent, as well as how to become a more effective communicator and how to coparent effectively with a positive purpose.

5. A regular time each week needs to be established for Becky (the mother) and Mark (the father) to communicate with each other regarding the children. The parents can negotiate the day and time for this weekly communication opportunity. It is both parents' responsibility to keep each other informed about the children's academic and extracurricular activities. Additionally, both parents need to keep the other informed about where the children are when they are in their care, as well as what their activities

will be and who is providing supervision for the boys. Jordan is not usually an appropriate child care provider for Dylan.

6. It is not in the children's best interest to have the parents continue their vendetta against each other. Both parents need to do self-exploration to better understand their need to "win" the children over to their side, to "win" over the other parent, and to "win" in proving what caused the breakup of the family. The children are the ones most affected by the continual fighting between Becky and Mark. Both parents need to put aside their needs for revenge to focus on becoming more effective coparents to better meet the needs of the children.

_____

Evaluator's name, degree, license, certifications   DATE

Another different example not previously mentioned:

3. Both parents and the stepparent would benefit from parent education/ divorce education classes. Possible referrals include the ABC Counseling Center (Good City) or classes offered by the Department of Children and Family Services in the geographic area of the parents.

4. Sally (the mother) would benefit from the services provided by the Center for Directions. The CFD provides career and personal counseling at no cost. The CFD is located on the USA University campus but also has a satellite center in the city where both parents live. It is important that Sally become financially independent in the near future.

5. Henry would benefit from counseling services. Counseling would provide Henry with a better understanding of his emotional issues and the role that alcohol plays in his life. It is assumed that neither parent will drink when he or she is caring for Victor.

6. Victor would benefit from being a member of an extracurricular team activity (e.g., tee ball, soccer, swimming). Victor needs the opportunity to realize that he can be a contributing member of a team. It is expected that both parents will facilitate Victor's involvement on this team and share the costs equally.

7. A regular time each week needs to be established for Sally and Henry to communicate with each other about Victor. The parents can negotiate the day and time for this weekly communication opportunity.

8. A reevaluation of this case may be necessary as Victor ages. It is hoped that Sally and Henry will have learned how to coparent and communicate effectively and can modify the custody and visitation schedule without a formal reevaluation. If a formal reevaluation is necessary, it should consider the coparenting and communications skills of both parents and whether the current custody and visitation schedule remains viable or whether a shared arrangement for visitation would better meet Victor's needs.

_____

Evaluator's name, degree, license, certifications   DATE

FINAL THOUGHTS

As you can see, recommendations can cover a variety of issues and concerns. Remember, these are just recommendations—the judge does not have to include them in the final order. However, these types of recommendations do provide possible ways to mitigate future issues between the parents and facilitate the positive growth of the child. These types of recommendations provide opportunities for the parents and the child to view themselves and their current situation differently. Well-written recommendations give hope to everyone involved in the breakup of the family, helping people believe that they can move their lives forward in a functional and appropriate direction.

Certainly there are other ways of writing reports. Some evaluators write in their report how they came to each recommendation. Some even write pages of justifications. No way is entirely right or wrong. You need to find your comfort zone in writing your reports. On one hand, if you include your professional reasoning in your report, it takes much longer to write the report and leaves you open for difficult court testimony if your reasoning is not well written. On the other hand, if you just write recommendations without any professional reasoning, that also leaves you open to a difficult time in court. Find a happy medium. As you read the recommendations given in the examples, discern the rationale behind the recommendations and how each one speaks to the best interest of the child.

Writing the report is challenging and time-consuming, but it is also a way to express your professional opinions in such a way that others outside the counseling profession can understand and reflect on your rationale for writing them. The more you write, the easier it will be and the better your reports will become. You will find that your reports will all include some recommendations that are similar, such as parents setting a time each week to communicate with each other about the child. You will also find that each report you write is unique to its particular case and the people connected to it.

MEDIATOR REPORT WRITING

The report written by a mediator is written in confidentiality and is straightforward: It states what the parents agreed to during mediation. The report often includes the agreement of custody and visitation along with the division of property and debts. The mediator's report is very detailed and rarely (possibly never) includes statements such as "the parents can negotiate the holiday schedule." Instead, the mediator's report spells out all the dates and times, by year, of the holiday schedule.

The mediator is writing his or her report for the judge, who ultimately will agree or disagree with the report regardless of the parent's agreement. It is the job of the mediator to help the parents agree to terms that a judge will also find suited to the child's best interest. The skill of the mediator and the quality of the report will be crucial to the final order the judge issues.

CASE MANAGER REPORT WRITING

The case manager does not usually submit regular written reports to the judge. The judge can order the case manager to write quarterly reports or even weekly reports to suit the judge's desire. Generally, the judge will want a final report from the case manager when the manager is excused from the case or the manager requests that the judge release him or her from his or her responsibilities as case manager.

The report the case manager writes gives a summary of the number of contacts by parent and by month. It also summarizes the type of complaints the parents brought to the case manager by month. The report will note whether the concerns changed or remained the same over time and whether the number of contacts decreased or increased over time. Any recurring problem times or dates are also noted. For example, if the number of contacts tended to increase just prior to the summer break for the child, perhaps the judge needs to issue orders remedying these concerns and thus eliminating the contacts with the case manager.

The report also lays out conclusions about the change in the parents' attitudes toward each other. It talks about the improvement (or lack thereof) of each parent's coparenting skills. It also notes improvement or negative growth in the child. In other words, the report gives the judge a summary of what is still wrong with the parents and what is better or worse about their parenting skills, as well as how these changes are affecting the child. The report also may give the judge some recommendations about future orders regarding mediation, evaluation, or case management.

The next chapter deals with writing reports dealing with unusual case dynamics such as very young children, relocating the children far away from one parent, updating an old case, and writing progressive visitation schedules.

8

Special Circumstances Cases

All the cases that come before an evaluator are difficult and high-conflict, but some cases bring special circumstances that pose additional dilemmas to the evaluator. Remember: All cases have unique qualities and must be dealt with by the evaluator on their own merits. However, some broad guidelines can help the evaluator whose case has additional special circumstances. The court is aware of these guidelines and understands that they can help guide an evaluator. First, we'll look at some general principles guiding all cases, including ones with special circumstances.

PARENTING PLANS: GENERAL GUIDELINES

1. The aim of any parenting plan is to provide stability for the child. A parenting plan does not aim to meet the parents' needs for fairness and equality, but rather to do what is best for the child.
2. Young children, especially those younger than age 3, need a parenting plan that preserves their primary attachment with their primary caregiver parent. Remember that a child with a healthy primary attachment then becomes able to have multiple healthy attachments.
3. A shared arrangement should be considered if both parents coparent effectively, have minimal conflict, and communicate with each other about the child's best interest without arguing. A shared arrangement works best when the parents work cooperatively

together and live close to each other (providing equal access to the same school, peers, and activities for the child).

4. Parental conflict is—if not the most negative factor—certainly one of the top reasons why a child fails to develop in a healthy and positive manner. Children who are exposed to long-term parental conflict are at high risk for later emotional disturbances. They are more likely to have academic problems; to be more aggressive, sexually active, anxious, depressed, and withdrawn; to abuse alcohol and other illegal substances; and to come into conflict with the juvenile and adult justice systems. Finally, as adults, they are more likely to have relationship problems ending in domestic violence, adultery, and divorce.

5. Healthy parenting plans build healthy relationships between the parents and the child. Moving too quickly, with lengthy or numerous visits, could have an opposite and disruptive effect on the relationship-building process.

6. A neutral exchange location may need to be considered if the parents cannot act courteously toward each other. If the parents are not willing to engage in conflict with each other at a neutral location, a neutral exchange plan may need to be developed at the daycare or school, or the parents may need to be professionally supervised.

7. Children all deal differently with their parents' separation and ultimate divorce. Any parenting plan needs to address the child's ability to cope with change and how he or she adjusts to the changes that are now part of his or her reality.

8. When there is more than one child, a different visitation schedule for each child may be necessary. A schedule that works well for a 5-year-old may not work for a 5-month-old. Regardless of different schedules, the children need to be together at regular times.

9. If a parent was not active in the child's life before the separation and had not developed a relationship with the child, the parenting plan should reflect a visitation schedule that starts with short regular contact that is increased as the relationship is built. As the parent–child bond is established and strengthened, the visitation schedule can be modified to reflect this change in relationship. A parent who has been away or absent for a lengthy period needs to build trust gradually and allow the child to get to know him or her.

The general guidelines are reasonable and not surprising to an evaluator. There are probably other guidelines you can think of that are also reasonable for all cases. These guidelines will help give structure to your recommendations, but they will not replace your counseling skills and your professional knowledge and judgments. There are other guidelines more specific to cases that involve a special and unusual circumstance such as the relocation of one parent far from the other parent, the presence of a very young child, the presence of children in the family with a wide range of ages, and updating a case over time.

PARENTING PLANS: VERY YOUNG CHILDREN

The challenges of writing recommendations for visitation are numerous. The recommendations must preserve the child's primary attachment with the primary caregiver, as well as provide for regular and consistent contact with the other parent in order to establish the bond between the parent and the child. Too much time away from the primary caregiver is not desirable, and too little time with the other parent is equally so. You must determine who the primary caregiver of the child is—but also whether that parent is capable of continuing in that role.

Don't automatically assume that the mother is the primary caregiver. It is equally likely that the father is the primary caregiver. Likewise, don't assume that the person who was the primary caregiver when the family was intact can maintain that same quality of care now. Determine whether the parent is actually doing the parenting—it may be that the grandparents or current girlfriend or stepparent is actually doing so instead. These issues have to be ferreted out during interviews. Also, evaluate the developmental appropriateness of the child and how attached the child is to each parent. Finally, evaluate the parent's ability to do the "grunt work" of caring for the child. Parents of children of all ages have to be able to feed them appropriately, clothe them, wash their clothes, bathe them, play with them, and care for them if they become ill. A parent of a young child has to be able to give up sleep for the child, comfort the child when he or she can't vocalize what is wrong, and provide the child opportunities to help the child develop trust and autonomy in his or her environment.

Guidelines to assist the court and evaluators in making age-appropriate recommendations for visitation schedules are generally broader as the child ages. Again, these are only guidelines, but they can be helpful to evaluators, attorneys, and parents.

Birth to 1 Year

1. Infants should live primarily with their primary caregiver.
2. Overnights are generally not recommended, but if both parents significantly participated in the child's care prior to the breakup of the family, overnights may be appropriate. One overnight a week could be recommended.
3. A child can have healthy attachments to others besides his or her primary caregiver. The attachments are formed with regular and consistent visits. These visits are generally short day visits that occur either daily, on alternate days, or at least two or three times a week.
4. The child's schedule must be considered when the visits occur. It makes no sense for the visits to occur when the child is sleeping.
5. Infants are especially attuned to conflict, so the schedule needs to minimize conflict or stress between the parents. If the parents cannot control themselves, then occurrences must be kept minimal.
6. As the bonding and relationship to the nonprimary caregiver strengthens, the visits can be longer. These visits should also take into account the child's schedule, and the visiting parent must maintain this schedule.

1 to 3 Years

1. Toddlers should reside with their primary caregiver most of the time.
2. Overnights are still not generally recommended. If the parents have both been consistently and actively involved in the care of the child, 1 overnight a week may be recommended.
3. Toddlers continue to need a rigid and predictable schedule. Day visits of 3 to 5 days a week are recommended for the visiting parent.
4. If there is conflict between the parents, the visits should be kept to a minimum. The exchange place for the visits may have to be at a neutral transition place without parent–parent contact.

5. The day visits can be most of the day if the child is able to tolerate that schedule.
6. If the visits are not regular and consistent, the visits should be 1 to 3 hours long.
7. Depending on the child and the parent's ability to maintain the child's schedule and avoid conflict with the other parent, overnights for a 3-year-old may be expanded to 2 nonconsecutive overnights each week. Extended vacation times and entire weekend visits are not recommended.

3 to 5 Years

1. Often 3- to 5-year-old children become fearful and anxious when separated from their primary caregiver for long periods. They may demonstrate behaviors consistent with this anxiety and fear when they transition from one parent's home to the other.
2. As the child becomes more comfortable moving between homes, additional time and 1 or 2 overnights can be recommended. This assumes that the visiting parent has had regular and consistent day visits with the child and that a bond has developed between that parent and the child.
3. It may be reasonable to consider splitting the weekends so the child has a full stay-at-home day and an overnight with each parent.
4. An alternate weekend visitation schedule and midweek contact could be recommended for the older children of this group if a significant bond exists with the visiting parent. It is assumed that this parent will be responsible for care for the child during the visits and the overnights.

6 to 8 Years

1. Again, a regular routine is important for children of these ages.
2. A visitation schedule should be flexible enough to include opportunities for the child to play with his or her friends and participate in his or her extracurricular activities. Both parents are responsible for facilitating these activities for the child.
3. Multiple overnights are generally acceptable.

4. A full week at either parent's home can be phased in by age 8. This assumes a significant bond between the child and his or her parents.
5. If the conflict is low between the parents and both parents live in close proximity to each other so that the child has access to the same school, friends, and activities, then a 60/40 visitation schedule can be recommended. Depending on the child, a shared arrangement may be appropriate.

9 to 12 Years

1. Many children this age desire one home base with specific weekends, evenings, and activities at the other parent's home.
2. Some children do well with a shared arrangement and may prefer that type of visitation schedule. Other children do not want the burden of changing homes each week. Regardless, a shared arrangement only works if there is little to no conflict between the parents. A workable shared arrangement requires each parent to coparent with the other parent reasonably and effectively. Communication between the parents must be consistent and workable between the parents for a shared arrangement to work.
3. Any schedule should be regular and predictable and minimize interference with the child's peer relationships, school, and extracurricular activities. Flexibility needs to be maintained in the visitation schedule to facilitate academic and extracurricular activities.

13 to 17 Years

1. Teens are capable and do form opinions about where they want to live. Their opinion should be considered but not necessarily followed.
2. Teens need some ownership in planning their schedule.
3. Some teens need a home base and regular time with the other parent. Others prefer and can handle a shared arrangement.
4. It is important for the teen to be able to maintain his or her access to academic and extracurricular activities and to his or her peers.

Besides these guidelines, you must also consider the case individually, including such things as the conflict between the parents; the parents' ability to coparent and communicate effectively with each other; the parents' current living arrangements; stepparents; stepsiblings; the child's ability to cope with stress, anxiety, and change; and the relationship the child has with each parent.

REPORT WRITING: RECOMMENDATIONS FOR YOUNG CHILDREN

Here are some examples of recommendations written for young children:

RECOMMENDATIONS FOR CUSTODY AND VISITATION OF ROBERTA PERSON

RE: PERSON VS PERSON (nka RICHARDS)

CASE NO.: CV-0000-000-DR

DATE: MARCH 10, 2014

1. Joint custody of Roberta Person be awarded to both parents, Randy Person and Beth Richards.
2. In light of Roberta's age, it is imperative that she have regular and consistent contact with both parents and a limited number of overnights away from her primary home:
   a) Roberta will live mostly with her father, Randy, while visiting regularly with her mother, Beth. Beth's visitation schedule would include caring for Roberta every weekday while Randy is at work. Additionally, Beth would have overnight visitation on alternate Saturdays from 11 a.m. to 4 p.m. Sunday. It is assumed that Beth would be the person providing the care for Roberta on the weekdays or weekends.
   b) Since Beth does not have a driver's license, Randy is responsible for the exchanges at Beth's home. Randy's wife, Julie, or his parents or another person acceptable to both parents can pick up or drop off Roberta.
   c) Holidays can be split or otherwise negotiated by the parents. Extended overnights with Beth are not recommended at this time.
   d) Beth is responsible for providing breast milk for Roberta if she continues to breastfeed.
3. Beth needs to be required to give Randy Roberta's Social Security number. This will allow him to access any of her records and provide medical insurance.
4. Randy's surname needs to be put on Roberta's birth certificate. It is recommended that Roberta's birth certificate reflect both parents' names and read Roberta Richards Person.

5. It is recommended that Beth not be permitted to leave the state of Illinois with Roberta. She is an illegal alien and thus needs to make every effort to become a legal resident. If Beth chooses to move to another state or country, she would leave Roberta with her father, and another visitation schedule would need to be agreed upon by the parents.
6. Beth needs to progress in learning English. Currently, she is unable to speak the language that Roberta will be required to speak when she enters school.
7. Beth needs to become employed full-time. Although this is a difficult thing to do because of her illegal status, she needs to become financially independent. Additionally, Beth needs to eventually live independently from family and friends and provide Roberta with an appropriate living environment.
8. A regular time each week needs to be established for the parents to communicate with each other regarding Roberta. The parents can negotiate this weekly communication opportunity.
9. Beth is currently receiving educational assistance from the Department of Health and Welfare regarding her older son. This assistance should be expanded to include Roberta as well.
10. A reevaluation of this case may be necessary as Roberta approaches school age. It is hoped that the parents can modify the visitation order without a formal reevaluation. If a formal reevaluation is necessary, it should consider Beth's alien status and ability to communicate in English, the coparenting skills of both parents, both parents' living arrangements and work schedules, and Roberta's best interests.

Evaluator's name, degree, license, certifications   DATE

As you can tell, there is more going on in this case than just the age of the child. Obviously, the child is an infant and thus needs the consistency of a primary caregiver and regular contact with the other parent. In this case, the father was judged to be the primary caregiver. Since the father works during the day and the mother does not, it was recommended that the mother care for the child while the father was at work.

Additionally, the evaluator determined that the mother could not give the stability or the environment necessary to meet the best interest of the child. Recommendations were made to promote the mother's future interests. Other recommendations were written to promote the father's and mother's abilities to coparent and communicate with each other effectively and to ensure that the child receives medical benefits and is not taken out of the state or the country.

Obviously, this was a very involved and difficult case. The conflict was high between the parents, especially on the mother's part. She continually made threats to the father about preventing him from seeing the child and her leaving with the child, as well as demands that were in her own interests but not the child's. The recommendations reflect what the evaluator believed would reduce the conflict while providing the child with a safe, consistent, and stable home.

Here's another example that involves a progressive visitation schedule in order to establish a relationship between the child and his or her nonprimary caregiver:

RECOMMENDATIONS OF CUSTODY AND VISITATION
OF JAMES GREEN

RE: GREEN VS GREEN

CASE NO.: CV-0000-000

DATE: FEBRUARY 22, 2014

1. Joint custody of James be awarded to both parents, Melanie Green and Steve Green. James's birth certificate should be corrected to remove Roy Land (a prior boyfriend of Melanie) and put Steve Green as the father.
2. It is recommended that James continue to live mostly with his mother, Melanie, while visiting regularly with his father, Steve:
   a) Steve will have visitation on alternate weeks on Monday, Wednesday, and Friday from 10 a.m. to 4 p.m. On the other alternate weeks, he would have visitation on Tuesday, Thursday, and Saturday from 10 a.m. to 4 p.m. The visitation assumes that Steve is available for providing care for James during his visitation.
   b) When James is 2½ years old, visitation would be Monday and Wednesday from 10 a.m. to 6 p.m. and Friday evening to Saturday evening. On the alternate week, visitation would be Tuesday from 10 a.m. to 6 p.m. and Thursday evening to Friday evening. The parents can negotiate the actual exchange times. It is assumed that Steve will be available for providing care for James.
   c) When James is 3½ to 4 years old, visitation would be Wednesday from 10 a.m. to 6 p.m. and Friday evening to Sunday evening. On alternate weeks, visitation would be Tuesday and Thursday from 10 a.m. to 6 p.m. The parents can negotiate the actual exchange times. It is assumed that Steve will be available for providing care for James.
   d) Regular phone contact between James and his parents needs to be established. The parents can negotiate the time for the daily phone contact.
   e) Travel would be shared equally between the parents.
   f) Holidays can be split or alternated as negotiated by the parents.
   g) Steve needs to obtain a valid driver's license or have someone else drive when he is caring for and exchanging James.

3. Both parents and stepparents would benefit from parent education/divorce education classes. The stepparents need to clearly understand their roles and boundaries and facilitate communication between James's parents. Possible referrals for the classes include the ABC Counseling Center and the XYZ Counseling Center.

4. Both Steve and Melanie would benefit from the services provided by the Center for Directions. The CFD is located on the America University campus and the AU campus in Atlas (where Melanie and Sam ["stepfather"] are planning on moving in the near future). The CFD provides personal and career counseling services at no cost. Steve needs to become employed as soon as possible to ensure his financial independence.

5. A time each week needs to be established for Steve and Melanie to communicate with each other regarding James. The parents can negotiate the day and time for this weekly communication opportunity.

6. A reevaluation may be necessary as James ages and Steve becomes employed. It is hoped that the parents will have established effective communication and coparenting skills by that time and can then modify the custody and visitation schedule without a formal reevaluation. If a reevaluation becomes necessary, it should consider both parents' ability to coparent and communicate effectively with each other, the parents' work schedules, and James's age-appropriate needs and best interest.

_____

Evaluator's name, degree, license, certificates   DATE

This case gives an example of a recommended visitation schedule for a young child who has no relationship with the nonprimary caregiver parent. The progressive schedule is more detailed and requires patience and considerable effort on the parents' part. It is not easy to establish a relationship with a child that is based on love, respect, and trust. Rushing to establish the relationship rarely, if ever, works for the child and the parent. The evaluator needs to carefully explain why the visitation schedule is so long and difficult so that the parent understands why he or she has to go through this process. It will pay off in the end, but getting there is difficult.

Additionally, the recommendations reflect what will help both parents and stepparents become better parents and coparents. This case recognizes that neither parent is financially stable and gives recommendations about how they can become employed. It also suggests referrals for divorce education classes for all the adults who are involved in this child's life. You can imagine the intricacies and the realities of this case and why the evaluator wrote the recommendations he or she did.

REPORT WRITING: RECOMMENDATIONS FOR GEOGRAPHIC DISTANCE BETWEEN THE PARENTS

Another special circumstance is when the parents live a significant distance from each other. Distance is not a friend to a child when it comes to regular and consistent contact. Generally, the court wants the child to see both parents often, but if the distance between the parents is prohibitive, the court must make rulings that take this into consideration.

PARENTING PLANS: GENERAL GUIDELINES FOR DISTANCE BETWEEN PARENTS

There are two divisions of distance: short (30 to 100 miles apart) and long (100+ miles apart). The general guidelines for visitation are similar to the guidelines for the other special circumstances cases.

The general guidelines for short distance visitation are as follow:

1. As always, what is fair and equal for the parents may not be what is best for the child. The best interests of the child are what are important.
2. Visitation schedules' main goal is developing a positive relationship between the parent and the child.
3. Lengthy visits, if they occur too quickly, can have a potentially disruptive effect on relationship building between the parent and the child.
4. Children differ in how they cope with change, stress, and anxiety. The visitation schedule needs to reflect these individual characteristics of the child in an attempt to alleviate the child's fear and anxieties.
5. When children of significantly different ages are in the family, there may be a need to have a different visitation schedule for each child. The schedules should attempt to keep the children together as much as possible while establishing schedules that are appropriate for their developmental levels.
6. If a parent has not played an active role in the child's life or has been absent from the child's life, the visitation schedule needs to provide for a slow building process so that the child and parent

can develop a bond with each other. This type of progressive visitation schedule allows for the formation of trust between the child and the parent.

7. Today's technology allows for the distant parent to maintain a closer relationship with the child. The use of technologies such as Skype, FaceTime, and instant messaging can make the time spent between the parent and the child more meaningful since they can actually see each other. Thus, the distant parent can participate in activities such as playing games, helping with homework, and reading books.

8. During any extended visitation time with the distant parent, the primary caregiver should be afforded the same type of regular contact with the child.

More specific guidelines come into play depending on the age of the child, as follows.

PARENTING PLANS: SHORT DISTANCE BETWEEN PARENTS

Birth to 18 Months

1. If the distant parent has had significant contact with the child, then it is recommended that he or she have 6 to 8 hours of consecutive visitation with the child. If he or she has not had significant contact with the child, the visitation should start with 2 consecutive hours, then continue to 3- and 4-hour blocks, building toward 6 to 8 consecutive hours.

2. The distant parent can have 1 overnight with the child if trust and bonding have occurred.

3. An extended number of overnights and vacations is not recommended for the distant parent.

18 Months to 3 Years

1. The suggested visitation time with the distant parent can be 2 consecutive day visits on alternate weeks, or more often if practical.

2. Visits should start with 2 consecutive day visits for up to 8 hours. If visitation with the distant parent is new or there is no positive

relationship built between the parent and the child, the visitation would be consecutive days with the distant parent for 4 consecutive hour-long blocks. The length of the visits would be expanded to 8 hours as a relationship is established between the parent and the child.

3. Visits can gradually increase to 1 overnight lasting from the morning of the first day until the late afternoon of the second day (e.g., 9 a.m. on the first day to 5 p.m. on the second).
4. Extended overnights and vacations are not recommended for this age group.

3 to 6 Years

1. Two to four consecutive overnights are generally tolerated by children in this age range.
2. If possible, the visitation should occur every 2 weeks from approximately 6 p.m. on the first day to 6 p.m. on the third or fourth day.
3. Regular phone contact is recommended since the child will probably not hold lengthy conversations. When the child is with the distant parent, he or she should have daily and regular access by phone to the primary caregiver parent.
4. Certain technologies such as Skype and FaceTime may improve the interaction between the child and parent during these regular phone contacts.

6 to 9 Years

1. Alternate weekend visits are appropriate for this age. Weekend visitation would be from 6 p.m. Friday to 6 p.m. Sunday.
2. Long weekends that occur during the school year can be included in the weekend visitation. For example, if there is a Monday holiday, the visitation would be 6 p.m. Friday to 6 p.m. Monday. If the holiday is on a Thursday, the visitation would be 6 p.m. Thursday to 6 p.m. Sunday.
3. Holidays can be split or alternated between the parents.
4. Summer visitation can total 3 to 4 weeks in 1- to 2-week blocks. Each block needs to be separated by at least 1 week with the primary caregiver parent.

5. Regular phone contact needs to be established between the child and the parents. During extended visitation, the child needs to have opportunities for regular contact with the primary caregiver parent.

9 to 16 Years

1. It remains appropriate for visitation to occur on alternate weekends from 6 p.m. Friday to 6 p.m. Sunday. Long weekends during the school year can also be included in the weekend visitation. For example, if Monday is a holiday, the visitation would be 6 p.m. Friday to 6 p.m. Monday.
2. Holidays can be split or alternated between the parents.
3. Summer visitation can be from 4 to 6 weeks. The visitation can be in 2- to 3-week blocks with at least 1 week in between spent with the primary caregiver parent.
4. Summer visitation can also be in a block of 4 to 6 weeks with the primary caregiver parent having alternate weekend visitation.
5. Regular phone contact needs to be established between the child and the parents. The child can initiate the calls, but both parents need to facilitate regular calls.

16 to 18 Years

1. The child's schedule for academic and extracurricular activities should be considered when establishing a visitation schedule. It would be the responsibility of whichever parent has the child at that time to facilitate his or her academic or extracurricular schedules. In other words, the parent who has the child is responsible for getting the child to his or her game or practice.
2. The visitation schedule needs to have flexibility to allow ownership by the child.
3. Holidays can be split or alternated.
4. Phone contact should be regular. The child can initiate the calls, but both parents need to facilitate regular calls.

There are also guidelines for long-distance visitation. The farther the parents are from each other, the more difficult visitation becomes, especially for younger children. The general guidelines for long distance between the parents are similar to those in the case of a closer distance between the parents, but more specific guidelines depend on age.

PARENTING PLANS: LONG DISTANCE BETWEEN PARENTS

Birth to 18 Months

1. When a child is an infant, if there is low conflict between the parents, it is recommended that one parent travel to the infant and visit at the infant's home. This will enable both parents to spend time with the child together. The primary caregiver parent can also travel with the infant to the visiting parent's home. The contact should occur at least once every 2 months.
2. The schedule should feature frequent but short visits—perhaps two visits a day for 1 to 2 hours each. The visitation can be gradually increased to two 4-hour blocks each day. This type of visitation can continue for several days in a row.
3. Out-of-state visits, lengthy overnight visits, and vacations with the distant parent are not recommended.

18 Months to 3 Years

1. Again, it is recommended that one of the parents travel in either direction to allow both parents to spend time with the child. This assumes that there is low conflict between the parents. It is recommended that contact occur at least once every 2 months.
2. The visits should be short: two visits a day for 3 to 4 hours each. Gradually increase the length of the visits for up to 8 hours once a day. After 3 consecutive days of 8-hour visits, 1 overnight can be added.
3. Out-of-state, lengthy overnights and vacations with the distant parent are not recommended.

3 to 6 Years

1. One of the parents needs to travel to the residence of the other parent.
2. Visitation can be 1 weekend each month consisting of no longer than a 2- to 3-day stay with the visiting parent. This may mean that the visit will occur in a hotel or the home of a local friend or relative.
3. It is recommended that the parents travel each month for visitation. If this is not possible, the parents can visit for up to 4 days in a row up to six times a year.

4. Regular phone contact needs to be established. It may be that the child does not talk a lot during the phone conversation; even so, the parent should call regularly anyway. When the child is with the distant parent, regular contact with the primary caregiver parent needs to occur. The use of technology such as Skype or FaceTime can enhance the contact between the parent and the child. Face-to-face contact allows the child to see the parent while talking with him or her. This technology also allows the parent to see the child and help him or her with homework and other activities.

6 to 9 Years

1. At this age, the child can probably tolerate out-of-state visitation with the distant parent.
2. The visits can be frequent, but no longer than 2 weeks' duration if the child can tolerate this extended time.
3. Summer visitation needs to be limited. An entire summer away from the primary caregiver parent is too long at this age.
4. Regular phone contact needs to be established both for the distant parent and for the primary caregiver parent when there is visitation. Technology such as Skype and FaceTime can make this contact more meaningful.

9 to 13 Years

1. Summer visitation can be increased to 4 to 6 consecutive weeks.
2. Additional holiday visitation may include half of Christmas break, half or all of Thanksgiving break, and all of spring break.
3. Regular phone contact needs to be established for both parents. Again, technology such as Skype and FaceTime can make this contact between the child and his or her parents more meaningful.

13 to 17 Years

1. Adolescents should be able to give their input into the visitation schedule. The child should not be given the ultimate authority to establish a visitation schedule but should be allowed to have input into the schedule.

2. The visitation schedule needs to incorporate the child's academic and extracurricular activities. The visitation schedule may need to be reviewed yearly.
3. The decision to visit or not visit the other parent should not be the child's.
4. Regular phone contact should be facilitated by both parents. The child can initiate the calls.

Here are some examples of recommendations written for parents who are not living close to each other. These cases are especially difficult when the children are young and cannot fly alone to visit the distant parent. Cases in which the parents live long distances from each other take a lot of commitment on both parents' parts to make sure the child has regular contact with the distant parent. It is also expensive for both parents to cover the costs of the travel, hotel, and so forth. One question that can help guide the recommendations is to ask yourself whether you would be willing to make that round-trip car ride on alternate weekends month after month. If not, then it probably isn't going to work for the child's best interests. It may well be that the parent has to do all the driving to be with his or her child at the child's home base.

RECOMMENDATIONS OF CUSTODY AND VISITATION OF THE BROWN CHILDREN

RE: BROWN VS BROWN (nka WHITE)

CASE NO.: CV-0000-000

DATE: DECEMBER 13, 2014

1. Joint custody of Sylvia, Stephanie, and Susan continue to be awarded to both parents, Bruce Brown and Linda White.
2. It is recommended that a visitation schedule be established that approaches a shared arrangement. It is recommended that the girls live mostly with their mother, Linda, during the school year and visit regularly with their father, Bruce:
   a) Both parents have agreed that Sylvia can determine her own visitation schedule with her father. At this time, Sylvia does not visit nor communicate with her father. Linda needs to encourage Sylvia to have at least a neutral relationship with her father. Bruce needs to consistently try to communicate with Sylvia through phone calls, cards, letters, and e-mails.
   b) During the school year, Bruce would have visitation with the girls for teacher in-service (October), fall break (including the weekends before and after the break), and spring break (including the weekends before

and after the break). He also would have visitation with the girls in South Dakota on every other 3-day weekend during the school year. It is his responsibility to inform Linda at least 2 weeks before his visitation in South Dakota. Visitation ends at a time and day that allow travel time and an appropriate number of hours for sleep (not in the car) before school begins. It is not acceptable for the children to miss school because they are traveling or have traveled all night to return to school. The parents can negotiate when visitation will end and delineate it in the parenting plan.

   c) Summer visitation would include 7 weeks in South Dakota with Bruce. Linda can visit the children in South Dakota on any 3 weekends from Thursday morning to Monday evening during the summer visitation time with their father. It is Linda's responsibility to inform Bruce of her visitation times in South Dakota at least 2 weeks before her visitation. The parents can negotiate the actual weeks when the girls will be with their father. Both parents need to consider Stephanie's dance commitments during the summer and to allow for the children to return to their mother 1 week before school begins.

   d) Thanksgiving holiday can be alternated between the parents. Christmas holiday can be split and the weeks alternated between the parents each year. Any other holidays can be negotiated between the parents.

   e) Regular and consistent phone contact between the children and their parents needs to be established. The parents need to facilitate this phone contact. The children can initiate the calls.

   f) Travel costs will be shared equally between the parents. Additionally, it is not acceptable for the children to take their suitcases with them to school on days when they go for visitation with their father. Either Bruce can pick the girls up at school and take them to Linda's home, where they can collect their suitcases, or Linda can meet Bruce and the girls at the end of the school day with the suitcases, and they can get them from her. Furthermore, it is recommended that flights to Sioux Falls from Bismarck be considered for travel for the girls between South Dakota and North Dakota.

3. Both parents and stepparents would benefit from parent education/divorce education classes. Referrals for classes in the South Dakota area could be obtained from the Department of Children and Family Services. Referrals for classes in North Dakota might also be obtained from a similar department.

4. Both girls are currently involved in extracurricular activities. The visitation with Bruce needs to take into account these activities. For example, during the summer Stephanie has dance camp. Thus, before setting the summer visitation schedule, both parents must have accurate information about the girls' activities and plan the girls' time in South Dakota accordingly. Additionally, both parents must proportionally share the costs of these activities.

5. A regular time each week needs to be established for Bruce and Linda to communicate with each other regarding the children. Currently, communication is done through e-mail or texts. Although this might continue

for the present, it is imperative that Linda and Bruce begin communicating with each other verbally in the near future in order to better coparent the children. The parents can negotiate the day and time for this weekly communication opportunity.

6. It is each parent's responsibility to keep the other parent informed about the children's academic and extracurricular activities. Neither parent has the right to not disclose information about the children to the other parent.

7. Linda and her current husband Larry need to become more financially independent. Both would benefit from the services provided by the Center for Directions. There is a CFD center in Bismarck at the North Dakota University Center. The CFD provides personal and career counseling at no cost.

Evaluator's name, degree, license, certifications   DATE

Here's another example:

RECOMMENDATIONS OF CUSTODY AND VISITATION OF THE RODRIQUEZ CHILDREN

RE: RODRIQUEZ VS RODRIQUEZ

CASE NO.: CV-0000-000-DR

DATE: APRIL 20, 2014

1. Joint custody of Juan Jr. and Carlos be awarded to both parents, Maria Rodriquez and Juan Rodriquez.

2. Maria is requesting a move away from American Falls, preferably to Caldwell (250 miles away) or, if not there, to Rockland (30 miles away). Because of her request to move, three options for custody and visitation are recommended:

OPTION 1

a) If Maria moves to Caldwell (250 miles away) it is recommended that the children live mostly with their father, Juan, while visiting regularly with their mother. Maria would have the children 1 weekend each month. This weekend would be a long weekend (e.g., teacher in-service, 3-day weekend). During the school year, there is one long weekend each month. Additionally, Maria would have visitation with the boys any time she was in American Falls. It would be her responsibility to inform Juan at least 48 hours before her visitation.

b) Maria would have summer visitation from 1 week after school ends until 1 week before school begins. Juan would have visitation 7 consecutive days in both June and July. Additionally, Juan would have visitation with the boys any time he was in Caldwell. It would be his responsibility to inform Maria at least 48 hours before his visitation.

c) Other holidays can be split or alternated as negotiated by the parents. It is recommended that the Christmas holiday be split and the weeks alternated each year between the parents. Spring break would generally be awarded to Maria.

d) Daily phone contact between the children and their parents needs to be established. The parents can negotiate the time for the daily phone contact. It is both parents' responsibility to facilitate this phone contact.

e) Travel cost would be shared equally by the parents.

OPTION 2

a) If Maria moves to Rockland (30 miles away), the children would live mostly with their father, Juan, and visit regularly with their mother. Maria would have visitation 3 overnights each week. The actual days would have to be determined by the parents after Maria finds out her work and school schedule. If Maria has the children during the school week, it would be her responsibility to deliver and pick up Juan Jr. from school.

b) Summer would remain the same with the addition of extended vacation time of 4 consecutive overnights (7 overnights total). It is the responsibility of whichever parent is using the extended time to inform the other parent at least 4 weeks before doing so.

c) Holidays could be split or alternated as negotiated by the parents.

d) Travel, except for Maria delivering and picking Juan Jr. up from school, would be shared equally between the parents.

e) Daily phone contact between the boys and their parents needs to be established. The parents can negotiate the time for this daily phone contact. It is both parents' responsibility to facilitate this phone contact.

OPTION 3

a) If Maria continues to live in American Falls, a shared arrangement is recommended. The shared arrangement would be a 4-day rotation between the parents. After Maria's work and school schedule is established, the parents can negotiate the actual days each parent will have the children. There has to be a degree of flexibility within the shared arrangement, because each semester Maria's school schedule will change and thus the actual days the children are with either parent will change. As the children age, the parents may agree to change the shared schedule to a week/week rotation.

b) Summer would remain the same, with the addition of 3 additional nights (7 consecutive overnights total). It is the responsibility of whichever parent is using the extended time to notify the other parent at least 4 weeks before doing so.

c) Holidays can be split or alternated as negotiated by the parents.

d) Daily phone contact between the children and their parents needs to be established. The parents can negotiate the time for this daily phone contact. It is both parents' responsibility to facilitate this phone contact.

3. The right of first refusal should be awarded to both parents. Additionally, both parents need to agree on child care providers for the children.
4. Both parents would benefit from parent education/divorce education classes. Possible referrals include the ABC Counseling Center and the XYZ Counseling Center.
5. Juan Jr. would benefit from being a member of a divorce therapy group. This type of group therapy is usually available through the school system at no cost. Carlos would also benefit from counseling services regarding his feelings concerning the divorce. Referrals include Dr. Smith (private practice—Caldwell) and the XYZ Counseling Center.
6. Maria would benefit from the services provided by the Center for Direction, located on the American University campus. The CFD provides personal and career counseling at no cost. The CFD can also assist her in enrolling in the nursing program at American University.
7. Both children would benefit from being a member of an extracurricular team activity such as soccer or tee-ball. Both children need to have the opportunity to belong and be a contributing member of a team. It is both parents' responsibility to facilitate these extracurricular activities. Both parents would share in any costs associated with these activities.
8. A day and time each week needs to be established for the parents to communicate with each other regarding the children. The parents can negotiate the day and time for this weekly communication opportunity.
9. A reevaluation may be necessary as the children age and their needs change. It is hoped that Juan and Maria will have established adequate coparenting skills by then to modify the visitation schedule themselves without a formal reevaluation. If a formal reevaluation becomes necessary, it should consider the parents' communication skills and coparenting skills; the growth of the children academically, socially, and emotionally; and any other pertinent considerations.

Evaluator's name, degree, license, certification   DATE

One more example:

RECOMMENDATIONS OF CUSTODY AND VISITATION
OF THE STEWART CHILDREN

RE: STEWART VS STEWART

CASE NO.: CV-0000-0000-OC

DATE: JUNE 1, 2014

1. Joint custody of Angela Stewart and Amy Stewart be awarded to both parents, Nathan Stewart and Jenny Stewart.

2. Jenny Stewart is requesting to move with the children to New Mexico. In light of the children's ages, Jenny's reasons for moving, and Nathan's work situation, Jenny's and the children's move away from the Twin City area to New Mexico is not recommended. Assuming that Jenny will stay in the Twin City area, the recommendations for custody and visitation include the following:

   a) A modified shared arrangement between Jenny and Nathan is recommended. The children will stay with their father, Nathan, on his days off work. One week, he would have the children for 2 overnights. The next week he would have 2 overnights, followed by 2 overnights with Jenny, then 3 more overnights with Nathan.

   b) Additionally, extended time for both of the parents of 3 additional overnights (6 consecutive overnights total) three times a year is recommended. It is the responsibility of whichever parent is using the extended time to inform the other parent at least 4 weeks before doing so. It is also assumed that during the extended time the parent will be available to care for the children.

   c) Regular phone contact between the children and their parents needs to be established. The parents can negotiate the time each day for the phone contact. It is both parents' responsibility to facilitate the phone contact.

   d) Holidays can be shared or alternated as negotiated by the parents.

   e) Both parents have the right of first refusal for child care.

   f) Neither parent will consume alcohol when caring for the girls.

3. Both Angela and Amy would benefit from regular, structured daycare/ preschool at least two times a week for 3 to 4 hours each time. Both girls need to better understand the concept of sharing and cooperation. Angela would benefit from Head Start when she is old enough to be registered.

4. Both parents would benefit from parent education/divorce education classes. Referrals for the classes include the ABC Counseling Center, the MNO Counseling Center, and XYZ Counseling, all located in Twin City.

5. Jenny would benefit from the services provided by the Center for Direction, located on the American University campus. The CFD provides personal, career, and academic counseling at no charge. The services provided by the CFD will help Jenny in enrolling in college and finding employment in an effort to become financially independent. Additionally, Jenny needs to find adequate housing for herself and the children.

6. Nathan needs to remain employed and to continue to pursue separate and adequate housing for himself and the children. He also needs to continue his sobriety.

7. A time each week needs to be established for the parents to communicate with each other regarding the children. The parents can negotiate the day and time for this weekly communication opportunity. Both parents need to develop and use effective communication and coparenting skills. The parent education/divorce education classes will help both parents in becoming more effective communicators and coparents.

8. A reevaluation may be necessary before Angela begins kindergarten. It is hoped that both Nathan and Jenny will have developed the skills necessary to communicate effectively with each other and that they can then modify the custody and visitation schedule themselves without a formal reevaluation. If a reevaluation becomes necessary, it should consider the coparenting and communication skills of both parents, the developmental stages of the children, the parents' current living arrangements, the parents' ability to support the children both emotionally and financially, and any other appropriate factors to facilitate the children's best interests.

Evaluator's name, degree, license, certification   DATE

Writing recommendations for children who are separated from one parent is a difficult task and one that takes professional thought and judgment on the part of the evaluator. There probably is no perfect solution to such a difficult problem. It is the job of the evaluator to look at the reality of the case and take into account who is the child's primary caregiver, the circumstances of both parents, and the age and developmental level of the child to decide what type of visitation schedule would help the child maintain a relationship with the distant parent. It is no easy task.

Equally difficult is when one parent requests to move farther away from the other parent. When both parents have a stable and consistent relationship with the child, it is not often in the child's best interest to change what is already working. The evaluator has to determine whether there is a compelling reason to change what has been working for the child. If one parent requests to relocate because the stepparent has a better job offer somewhere else, is that a compelling reason to change the parenting plan and restrict contact with the other parent? It may not be. If one parent requests a move because he or she wants to live closer to his or her family, is that a compelling reason to take one parent out of a child's life on a regular basis? Probably not. Every case has its own set of characteristics and nuances that must be considered by the evaluator; ultimately, however, the evaluator has to write recommendations that are in the child's best interest and must consider whether the reasons for moving or changing the level of contact with one parent are compelling.

PARENTING PLANS: UPDATE

Now let's shift to another type of special circumstance. Often the original evaluator is asked to update his or her report after a relatively lengthy period has passed or the parents' circumstances have changed significantly. Updating a report is, on the one hand, easier than writing the original report but, on the other hand, may pose hidden difficulties for the evaluator.

Step 1

The first step is reviewing the notes from the original evaluation to refresh your memory of the case and remember why you wrote the recommendations you did. The value of good notes is now more apparent than ever. If your notes are written in such a way as to detail the parents' concerns and the child's perspectives, refreshing your memory of the case will not be difficult. If your notes are poorly written and lack detail, your memory may not be able to make up their shortcomings. Before beginning the update, have a firm grasp of what happened during the original evaluation, as well as of all other pertinent facts. It is not efficient or effective to begin from the beginning.

Step 2

Next, decide who you are going to interview again. Generally, the parents are re-interviewed, but the child may or not be. It is usually in the child's best interest to be kept away from the legal process as much as possible. However, if a teenager or a preteen is requesting to change primary residences, it is reasonable to reinterview the child to discover his or her motivation. Alternately, if a young child is being used by both parents as a pawn in their attempt to change the parenting plan, he or she may not give you any other useful information. If the child has been in counseling, it is reasonable to consult with the child's counselor to get information about the child. After that conversation, the evaluator can make a better judgment about whether to reinterview the child. Keeping the child out of "adult business" is often a good idea.

Collateral Contacts

The evaluator also needs to decide what collateral information he or she will review and with whom he or she will talk. Depending on the case, the collateral contacts and information may be none, some, or many. Consider only the collateral contacts and information that will enhance your understanding of what has changed since the original evaluation and that can help you in making updated recommendations.

Cost

The cost of an update is generally less than the cost of the original evaluation. You have previously based your charge for an update on the time it will take and the amount of work required. Be sure to add in the time it takes to review the past information to get you up to speed. Because the cost of the update is generally less, the interview time is shorter for the parents. The original interviews were approximately 2 hours with each parent, but the update interviews could be about 1 hour apiece. The exact duration will, of course, depend on the circumstances of the case. Usually, there is no appointment for the parent to engage in an activity with the child. Again, if the case demands that kind of an appointment, then it would be scheduled and the cost of the update adjusted accordingly. Often the interview with the child (if applicable) is also shortened. Overall, updates should take less time than the original evaluation.

Report Writing

After you have conducted the interviews and have considered all the information, look over the original recommendations again and decide whether there are compelling reasons now to change any of the recommendations already submitted to the court. Often some recommendations can remain the same. Others might need to be eliminated or changed depending on the information you gathered during the update. Take some time to think about your new recommendations before you begin to write. Then update your report to the court.

The updated report briefly reports on each interview and on what collateral contacts were made, along with any new information reviewed for the updated report. Any recommendations that remain the same from the first report can be described with reference to their number in the original report. Any recommendations changed or removed from the first report need to be detailed in the updated report. Remember: To make changes to the original report, you must have compelling reasons for the changes. Has one parent become employed out of state and thus unavailable to care for the child in a shared arrangement? Has one parent become incarcerated? Has one parent remarried, and are the stepsiblings and stepparent unwelcoming to the child? Has the child begun to demonstrate behaviors that suggest that the current visitation schedule is no longer meeting his or her needs? There can be any number of reasons for changing your recommendations, but be sure they are compelling enough to change what is working well for the child.

Here's an example of an original report, then its first update, followed by its final update. You can see how some of the recommendations remained the same and how others changed as a result of changed circumstances in the parents' lives.

UPDATED REPORT EXAMPLES

Original Report Example:

RECOMMENDATIONS OF CUSTODY AND VISITATION
OF THE ADAMS CHILDREN

RE: ADAMS (nka ADKINS) VS ADAMS

CASE NO.: CV-0000-0000-DR

DATE: MARCH 23, 2014

1. Joint custody of Ben Adams, Carey Adams, and Jayden Adams be awarded to both parents, Betty Adkins and Frank Adams.
2. On a temporary basis, a shared arrangement of custody and visitation is recommended. The shared arrangement would be a week/week rotation between the parents:
   a) Currently both parents are living in the family home with the children. It is recommended that one of the parents, either Betty or Frank, move from the family home and obtain his or her own home for himself or herself and the children. The parents can negotiate which one of them will move at this time.
   b) Holidays can be shared or alternated as negotiated by the parents. It is recommended that the Christmas holiday be split and the weeks alternated each year. Spring break can be split or alternated as negotiated by the parents.
   c) Summer would remain the same as the school year with the addition of extended time of 7 additional overnights (2 consecutive weeks) for each parent. It is the responsibility of whichever parent is using the extended time to inform the other parent at least 4 weeks before doing so. It is assumed that the parent using the extended time will be available to care for the children during the extended time.
   d) Regular phone contact needs to be established between the children and their parents. The parents can negotiate the time each day when the phone contact will occur. It is both parents' responsibility to facilitate the phone contact.
   e) Both parents would have the right of first refusal for child care.
3. Both parents would benefit from parent education/divorce education classes. Possible referrals include the ABC Counseling Center and the XYZ Counseling Center.

4. Ben especially would benefit from counseling services to help him better understand his role as a child in a divorced family. Possible referrals include the ABC Counseling Center, the XYZ Counseling Center (Dr. Smith as the counselor), or Dr. Paul (private practice in Good City). The school often offers a divorce group for children, and this also would be appropriate.

5. All the children would benefit from being involved in extracurricular activities of their choice. Participating in extracurricular activities provides opportunities for the children to view themselves as having other positive attributes to offer in arenas other than academics. All the children are currently involved in extracurricular activities, and this should continue. The parents can share the costs of these activities.

6. Jayden should be evaluated for speech therapy services. The request for the evaluation can be made through the school system. Additionally, Jayden would benefit from being in an organized preschool or in Head Start next year.

7. A time each week needs to be established for the parents to communicate with each other regarding the children. The parents can negotiate the time and day for this weekly communication opportunity. Additionally, each parent is responsible for informing the other of his or her correct physical address and a phone number that he or she will answer in a timely fashion. Further, each parent needs to remain vigilant in not involving the children in the "adult business" of the divorce or talking poorly of the other parent in front of the children.

8. Frank needs to become employed as soon as possible. His employment schedule will need to be considered during the reevaluation.

9. A reevaluation needs to be conducted prior to the beginning of the 2013 to 2014 school year. The reevaluation needs to consider both parents' ability to communicate and coparent effectively with each other and the parents' work schedules and living arrangements. Furthermore, it needs to consider whether the shared arrangement continues to be appropriate for the children or whether another custody and visitation schedule would better meet the children's needs. The reevaluation could also determine whether the shared custody and visitation schedule or an alternate custody and visitation schedule should remain temporary or become permanent at that time.

Evaluator's name, degree, license, certification   DATE

First updated report example:

UPDATED RECOMMENDATIONS OF CUSTODY AND VISITATION
OF THE ADAMS CHILDREN

RE: ADAMS (nka ADKINS) VS ADAMS UPDATE #1

CASE NO.: CV-0000-0000-DR

DATE: AUGUST 11, 2014

1. Joint custody of Ben Adams, Carey Adams, and Jayden Adams be awarded to both parents, Frank Adams and Betty Adkins.
2. Currently, visitation is on a temporary basis and consists of a shared arrangement of a week/week rotation between the parents. The realities of this case warrant a continuation of the temporary shared arrangement. Frank is currently living with his parents and remains unemployed. There is uncertainty about when and where he will obtain employment. He has applied for several jobs, some of which are not in Good City. Until the employment issue is resolved, his work schedule established, and he is able to live independently, there are no compelling reasons to move toward a permanent custody and visitation schedule at this time:
   a) Holidays can be shared or alternated as negotiated by the parents. It is recommended that the Christmas holiday be split and the weeks alternated each year. Spring break can be split or alternated as negotiated by the parents.
   b) If a permanent custody and visitation schedule has not been established by the summer of 2014, then summer visitation would remain the same as the school year with the addition of extended time of 7 additional overnights (2 consecutive weeks) for each parent. It is the responsibility of whichever parent is using the extended time to inform the other parent at least 4 weeks before doing so. It is assumed that the parent using the extended time will be available to care for the children during the extended visitation time.
   c) Regular phone contact needs to be established for the children to communicate with their parents. Each parent will establish a time each day for the children to talk with the other parent. It is each parent's responsibility to make the children available, give them privacy, and provide a phone so they can talk each day to the other parent. All the children need to have daily contact with both parents. This contact needs to happen each day and should not be left up to the children's discretion.
   d) Both parents would have the right of first refusal for child care.
3. It is imperative that the children's lives remain as similar as possible to their lives before the divorce. Thus, it is recommended that the children attend the same school (Whittier Elementary) they have always attended and participate in the same activities in which they have always participated (e.g., the same scout troop).
4. Recommendations 3–8 listed on the original evaluation, dated March 23, 2013, continue to remain viable and are recommended still.
5. A reevaluation should be conducted after Frank has become employed, has an established work schedule, and is providing adequate housing (independent from his parents) for himself and the children. The reevaluation would also consider both parents' ability to communicate and their ability to coparent with each other. The reevaluation would consider whether a shared arrangement continues to meet the children's

needs or whether another custody and visitation schedule needs to be established.

_____

Evaluator's name, degree, license, certification   DATE

Second updated report example:

UPDATED #2 RECOMMENDATIONS OF CUSTODY AND VISITATION OF THE ADAMS CHILDREN

RE: ADAMS (nka ADKINS) VS ADAMS UPDATE #2

CASE NO.: CV-0000-0000-DR

DATE: APRIL 1, 2015

1. Joint custody of Ben Adams, Carey Adams, and Jayden Adams continues to be awarded to both parents, Betty Adkins and Frank Adams.
2. There has been substantial change in Frank's situation since the last update. He has found full-time employment in Good City and has remarried. He is now a stepparent to two children, aged 10 and 12. He and his family are now living independently, no longer in his parents' home. In light of these changes in circumstances, it is recommended that the temporary custody and visitation schedule become permanent with some recommended changes:
   a) Summer visitation would remain the same with the addition of extended time of 7 additional nights (2 consecutive weeks) for each parent. It is the responsibility of whichever parent is using the extended time to notify the other parent at least 4 weeks before doing so. It is assumed that the parent using the extended time will be available to care for the children during the extended visitation time.
   b) Holidays can be shared or alternated as negotiated by the parents. It is recommended that the Christmas holiday be split and the weeks alternated each year. Spring break can also be split or alternated as negotiated by the parents.
   c) Regular phone contact needs to be established for the children to communicate with their parents. Each parent will establish a time each day for the children to talk to the other parent. It is each parent's responsibility to make the children available, give them privacy, and provide a phone so they can talk each day to the other parent. The daily phone contact needs to happen each day and should not be left up to the children's discretion.
   d) Both parents have the right of first refusal. Additionally, both parents need to agree on who is providing child care. Currently, they have agreed to allow Mary, the stepmother, to provide child care for all the children.
3. It is still important for the children's lives to be consistent with their lives before the divorce. It is recommended that the children continue to attend

their same schools. Next year, Ben moves into middle school. He prefers to go to Franklin Middle School, where his friends from Whittier Elementary School will be attending. Furthermore, both parents have put tremendous pressure on Ben to change scout troops or decide on his own what troop he wants to be a part of; he has chosen to finish this year with his old troop and then stop scouting. I support his decision. Carey continues to want to attend her current school next year. I also support this decision.

4. Ben is currently receiving counseling services from the school counselor and this needs to continue. It may be necessary to provide private counseling for Ben over the summer. Possible referrals include Dr. Smith at the XYZ Counseling Center or Dr. Paul or Mr. Jones at ABC Counseling. The parents would share the costs equally.

5. All the children are engaged in extracurricular activities. These activities are important for the children's continued positive development. Both parents would share the costs of these activities equally.

6. Jayden and Carey need to be evaluated for speech therapy services. The request for the evaluation for both children can be made through the school system.

7. Jayden should be enrolled in Head Start or another organized preschool such as Montessori. Both parents would share the costs equally.

8. A regular time each week has been established for the parents to communicate with each other about the children. Although there are times when Frank and Betty struggle with their communication skills, the weekly communication opportunities have eliminated some misunderstandings between the parents, allowed for information to go between the parents regarding the children's schedules and academic progress, and given the parents the opportunity to attempt to be successful coparents. Even so, there still are times of rudeness toward each other and attempts to make simple transactions difficult.

9. Each parent needs to make a concerted effort to avoid speaking poorly about the other parent in front of the children, involving the children in the details of the divorce and other "adult" business, focus on spending quality time with each of the children, and avoid concentrating more on his or her needs than on the needs of the children.

10. A reevaluation may be necessary as the children age. It is hoped that the parents can communicate and coparent effectively with each other by that time sufficiently to negotiate modifications to the custody and visitation schedule without a formal reevaluation. If a formal reevaluation becomes necessary, it should consider whether the shared arrangement of custody and visitation remains viable in light of the parents' ability to coparent and communicate effectively with each other and any other factors relevant to the children's best interests.

Evaluator's name, degree, license, certification   DATE

Here is another example of an updated report:

UPDATED RECOMMENDATIONS OF CUSTODY AND VISITATION OF THE WADA CHILDREN

RE: WADA VS WADA UPDATE

CASE NO.: CV-0000-0000-DR

DATE: FEBRUARY 14, 2014

The original recommendations of custody and visitation were completed October 23, 2012. There are no compelling reasons at this time to substantially change the original recommendations. The parents continue to use a shared week/week arrangement. This schedule works for the children. However, both parents can make changes in their coparenting to better facilitate this shared arrangement:

a) The parents have not established a time each week to communicate with each other about the children. It is imperative that this communication opportunity be established and that the parents commence talking to each other in an adult and businesslike fashion. Both parents need to accept responsibility for the children and actively engage in this weekly communication session. This time is not to be used to censor the other parent's behaviors or lifestyle, but rather to build a united front for the children.

b) Neither parent will speak poorly about the other parent in front of the children. The children are hypervigilant in listening for each parent to speak ill of the other. Each parent will maintain neutrality, positive comments, or silence in speaking about the other parent.

c) Each parent needs to be consistent in spending significant one-on-one time with the children. It is clear that the children misbehave and become defiant as a way to draw attention to themselves and provoke their parents to pay individual attention to them. Mark particularly needs to be especially conscientious about spending special time with his children. The number of children living in his home may make it easy for a child to feel lost, unappreciated, and unnoticed there.

d) Although there has been some improvement in the parents' abilities to coparent effectively, there is still room for improvement. Each parent must learn to talk to the other effectively, appreciate what the other has to offer the children, stop judging the other's life choices, and present a unified front of two parents working together in the best interests of the children.

_____

Evaluator's name, degree, license, certification   DATE

As you can see, updated reports vary in length and detail. Some updated reports substantially change the original recommendations;

others make very few changes. Updates look for compelling reasons to make changes after the passage of time. The updated evaluation determines whether what is currently happening is working well for the child.

Updated reports allow the court to see how well the original order is meeting the best interests of the child. It provides the court with the information it needs to make changes, whether substantial, cosmetic, or not at all, to the order of custody and visitation. It gives information allowing the court to assess whether the parents are making a concerted effort to coparent with each other and whether the child is developing positively both emotionally and psychologically. Updated reports are always helpful to the court viewing the case in the present.

Updates also give the parents feedback about their efforts to become the coparent their child needs in this situation. It lets the parent know what he or she is doing well and in what areas he or she needs to continue improving. It also gives the parent a perspective on how things have changed for his or her child and himself or herself as time has passed. The updated report describes not only the negative things that are still happening, but also the areas that have shown improvement.

PARENTING PLANS: PARENTAL ALIENATION

The last special circumstance is parental alienation. Many texts and studies have dealt with this phenomenon. It is the responsibility of every evaluator to know and understand what parental alienation is and is not. Generally, parental alienation occurs over time when one parent makes a concerted and continual effort to turn the child away from the other parent. But parental alienation is easier to describe than to recognize. The evaluator needs to know when the parent's behavior is actual alienation and when it is behavior common to all high-conflict cases.

In every high-conflict case that comes before an evaluator, neither parent is acting like a reasonable adult, and each carries much intense emotion when it comes to the other parent. This is to be expected. Each parent will talk poorly about the other in front of the child. Usually, one parent does this with more regularity, but when the breakup is new and the legal system is mostly controlling the case, both parents are running primarily on anger, resentment, sadness, anxiety, and hope for revenge. This is what happens in such cases; it does not mean the evaluator should label these behaviors parental alienation.

Before you begin calling out parental alienation, stop and consider whether a parent is actually engaged in a regime of alienation or simply acting as most parents do in a high-conflict case. If you see parental alienation, then label it as such, but do not use that label lightly and often without regard to which behaviors are expected under the circumstances.

The recommendations of the evaluator help the court identify problem areas that could affect the positive development of the child. If you accuse one parent of using parental alienation strategies, then your recommendations must go on to address how the court needs to respond to eliminate the negative impact of these behaviors on the child. It does not do the parents, the child, or the court any good for you to make no realistic recommendations for counteracting the behavior. Think deeply about the case before you apply any labels to either parent, and then be ready to provide the court with realistic options for dealing with the inappropriate behaviors—and be prepared to defend your labeling to both attorneys and the court during testimony.

SUMMARY

All the cases that come before an evaluator have their own special characteristics. That is why each case has to be dealt with on its own merits. There are no specific recipes that work for every case. There are guidelines that can help the evaluator, but in the end, you must use your own professional judgment and experience in writing recommendations. Special circumstances that may be involved in some cases make your job even more difficult: Deal with them with thoughtfulness and care. Base your recommendations on the reality of the case, dealing with all special circumstances. If you write your recommendations with the best interests of the child as their primary focus, considering special circumstances and offering reasonable solutions counteracting their negative effects on the child, the court will appreciate your assistance and be inclined to write orders reflecting your recommendations for the best interest of the child.

9

Working Through a Case

Let's try working through an actual case. At this point, you understand what to look for when conducting interviews and reviewing notes, listening with your counseling ear to hear not only what the person says but the meaning behind his or her words. You are hearing his or her story, but also his or her feelings and motives. It is your job to collect enough information to paint the picture of this family while they were together and now that they are apart.

You are the child's voice in court. It is your job to help the court issue the best possible order of custody and visitation for the child. Your professional experience and opinion will help set the direction for this child's life, emotional well-being, and positive development. It is a big responsibility.

Remain calm, cool, and collected throughout this process. Don't jump to conclusions before you have all the information you need to make reasonable recommendations. Don't become emotional, dramatic, or excessive. Remember that these people are coming to you engaged in a high-conflict situation: They are going to be angry, sad, vengeful, and not particularly introspective.

Now read this actual case. The names have been changed to protect the participants' identities. Dates have also been changed, but the time between appointments and so forth remain consistent with what actually happened. The notes are handwritten, having been produced during interviews. As with all case studies, some information is missing because you weren't there to experience the sessions. After some questions for you to consider, any pertinent information that has not been given will be provided to give you a better understanding of what happened during the sessions. Afterward, read the recommendations that were provided to the court and compare them to your own.

THE CASE OF SMITH VS SMITH

RE: SMITH VS SMITH

CASE NO.: CV-2010-0000-DR

DATE: JANUARY 1, 2010

A court order, a generic order appointing an evaluator, arrived in your mail on January 5, 2010. Both parents involved in the case, Ann Smith and Bob Smith, have contacted your office to set up appointments for their evaluations, using the contact information provided on the court order. The names and addresses of both attorneys were also included, along with the name of the judge assigned to this case. In short, the order gives you the authority to talk with anyone, and collect any information, deemed relevant to making recommendations concerning the custody and visitation of the minor children. As the evaluator assigned to this case, you will interview both parties, the minor children, and any other pertinent collateral contacts, as well as review school, medical, mental health, and any other records requested. Additionally, you will convey your recommendations to the court as soon as possible and refrain from ex parte communication with attorneys. The cost of the evaluation will be split equally between the parties and the cost of court testimony will be borne by the requesting party.

MOTHER'S INTERVIEW

The first appointment was on January 22, 2010. The mother, Ann Smith, came to the office alone for her interview. The interview started with a discussion about the lack of confidentiality in legal cases, what to expect from this interview, and the purpose of the interview. Discussion of money (already done once on the phone when the appointment was set up) and the future appointment with the mother and the children took place in more detail at the end of the interview. In addition, the evaluator clarified the names and ages of the children, the name of the mother's attorney, the name of the father's attorney, and whether the mother or the father was currently living with anyone who was providing stepparenting for the children. All these details were also discussed when the appointment was established.

Ann was a reasonable person; she was dressed appropriately, able to communicate effectively, and not apparently under the influence of drugs or alcohol. She understood the evaluation process and was anxious to begin. She said she was nervous about the appointment (which is expected) but seemed to be able to collect her thoughts and tell her side of the story of the family before the breakup, during the breakup, and after the breakup, including now. She was a nice person and seemed reasonable considering her current circumstances.

The following notes were generated during Ann's interview and will tell much about Ann, her parenting abilities, and her perspectives on the children and her soon-to-be ex-husband. Read them and then think about what you have read before you answer the questions that follow. At the end of the interview, Ann paid for her share of the evaluation and was given a receipt. There was a discussion about what this money paid for and what other costs might be incurred if the evaluator was asked to actually testify in court. An appointment was set up for Ann to bring the children. There was a discussion about what to tell the children about why they were coming to see the evaluator and about what was going to happen during the session with the children while they were with their mother and when they were alone with the evaluator. Also discussed was the process the evaluator followed in submitting the recommendations to the attorneys and the court and a probable timeline for completion of the case. Ann was asked whether she wanted to say anything else or talk about anything not already discussed. The interview with Ann lasted 2 hours:

Mother's Interview Notes

Director Family
at ____ Solutions
← working w/ obedience autism flexible schedule

1-22-10   Ann Smith

Ann Smith
(Mrs. W.A.) attorney's name

married Bob - June 2004
Bob: drinking heavily
domestic violence
OCD. very controlling - no messes - no
children crying
wanted his family to appear perfect
to outside world -

Bob Smith
attorney's name

Sam witnessed Bob choking her, hitting
bloody her - 8 months preg. w/.

Bob kicks in Sam's door - she tries
to leave w/ Sam."

8 Months

She goes back to him w/ his promises to not
drink
- he continues to drink
- having affairs

divorced
Steve Smith

March 9, 2009 - confronts him about girlfriend
- seperates

Bob: moved in w/ Linda

2

Bob: had children alt. wkends F-S
in family home

alt. wk 5:30-8:30 PM

End March 2009 - took children to Linda's
house - refused to return them
to mom
- finally returned children on Sunday

- Police called DV in Dec. - Bob threatened
her to stop call

- Bob - moke into house several times
His behavior became more erratic - refused
to return children - Bob kept children from him 1 month
Temporary Order) - just before Thanksgiving 2009

1. Steve - 8am-6pm - every Sat. & Sun - Dad
dad - 8am; Thurs 6pm - Sunday every wkend

- Bob - currently living w/
Linda and her 4 children

2. Special Master ordered -

(continued)

3

Sam — 3 - kindergarten — elem. City School
- worries about mom / dad
- very anxious child
- hates changes
- hates surprises
- afraid to be lost, afraid mom wouldn't
  come and get him
  - severe separation anxiety
  - scared child
currently - pees pants 2-3X day
      constantly checking on where
      mom is
    - poops pants - mostly at dad's
      house
sleeps in own bed - then comes in to
  mom's bed - wants to hold mom's hand
  - nightmares
      some about lindis re getting
      out of prison
      being left out of either
      family

does well in school
has friends -
    dad refuses to take him to any
    activities when he has

4

Sam currently in eshing
— Debbie
XXX Esling
— alt. Fridays – 3-4 months)
does go to xx daycare better when Steven goes)

Steve – 19 months –
Happy baby
some separation anx –
— currently going to daycare) xxxdaycare
walking
single words)
understands receptive lang. – understands)
sign language

— Ann can do random UA's for drugs/
alcohol –

Issues – Sam –

1. Mom primary
Dad visitation – alt. wkends F-SL)
alt. wks evening visits –
day visits ⚡5:S

(continued)

5

3. Summer Same schedule
   maybe short extended visits

4. Holidays —

- Linda   - 4 children, 4 different fathers
   - web sites of nude pics. of her
   Sam says she disciplines my her
   -- made to eat unwanted food
   - she & her children have moved 4–5.
   times
   - she & Bob have moved 2 times

she drives by - flips her off - yells bitch at
   her on drive-bys

- Sam comes home w/ inappropriate
   moves - thrusting, stripping
- uses her 13 yr. old daughter as babysitter
   5:1 ratio

no step parenting philosophy
   she likes confrontation - tries to
   instigate fights —

(continued)

> *He will say —*
>
> *She had an affair*

Questions to Consider: Mother

Here are some questions to consider after reading the notes generated during the mother's interview. Remember: These do not tell the entire story—just Ann's side of it.

1. What, in Ann's perspective, was the family like prior to the breakup?
2. How would you describe the relationship Ann and Bob had during their marriage?
3. Who was the primary caregiver during the marriage?
4. Were alcohol or drugs a problem in the marriage?
5. Was either parent unfaithful during the marriage?
6. Why did they separate?
7. What were the arrangements for visitation after the separation?
8. Where are the parents currently living?
9. Are there any temporary visitation orders in place?
10. Are the temporary orders working for the children?
11. What is Sam (the oldest child) like? How does his mother describe him? What are her concerns about Sam?
12. What is Steve (the youngest child) like? How does his mother describe him? What are her concerns about Steve?
13. How does Ann describe Linda (the stepparent)? How do the children get along with Linda?
14. What are Ann's desires for custody and visitation for the children?
15. What are the chances of Ann and Bob becoming reasonable coparents?

Now that you have answered the questions, let's see how closely your answers match the evaluator's. Remember: You are at a disadvantage since you weren't at the interview. However, your responses to the questions might be as valid as or even better than the evaluator's answers—in any case, there should be some similarity between your responses and the evaluator's.

Questions to Consider: Mother/ Evaluator's Answers

1. **What, in Ann's perspective, was the family like prior to the breakup?**
   The relationship between Ann and Bob was not a serene one. There was domestic violence against Ann by Bob even in front of the oldest child. To the outside world, the relationship appeared a good one: Both parents were educated and employed and raised the children as a unit. However, as in many relationships, the reality of the family was significantly different behind closed doors. Ann behaved as is often common for a victim of domestic violence, becoming pregnant with a second child and believing Bob when he said that he would never hit her again, that he would stop drinking, and so forth. Ann tried to save the marriage for as long as she could, but when she found out about Linda, she confronted Bob about the affair. It was then that Bob moved out of the family home and into Linda's home.

2. **How would you describe the relationship Ann and Bob had during their marriage?**
   The relationship was one of some good times but many bad. Bob drank to excess and became violent. He choked Ann, hit her, and engaged in other physical attacks, such as breaking doors and hitting walls.

3. **Who was the primary caregiver during the marriage?**
   Ann was the primary caregiver of the children, but Bob did interact with the children. He would take them to child care and pick them up. But he also physically abused Ann in front of their oldest son.

4. **Were alcohol or drugs a problem in the marriage?**
   Ann calls Bob an alcoholic. She further claims that when he drank he drank until he was intoxicated and became violent with her—but not the children.

5. **Was either parent unfaithful during the marriage?**
   Ann claims that Bob was unfaithful during the marriage and is now living with his girlfriend and her four children.

6. **Why did they separate?**
   There were two good reasons: the domestic violence and the girlfriend. Ann separated from Bob when she discovered the girlfriend.

7. **What were the arrangements for visitation after the separation?**
   Originally, Bob had the children on alternate weekends from Friday to Sunday in the family home. Ann left the home when he cared for the children. Eventually, he took the children to where he was living with Linda and kept them there with him. Ann claims he wouldn't return the children until the end of his weekend visitation. A temporary order was issued just before Thanksgiving: Bob was to have visitation with the youngest child, Steve, every Saturday and Sunday from 8 a.m. to 6 p.m. He would have

Sam, the oldest child, every Thursday to Sunday. Ann had no weekends with the children under the terms of the temporary order.

8. **Where are the parents currently living?**

   Ann currently lives in the family home; Bob lives together with his girlfriend and her four children.

9. **Are there any temporary visitation orders in place?**

   The temporary orders mentioned in point 7 have been in effect for approximately 2 months.

10. **Are the temporary orders working for the children?**

    The oldest child is suffering from the breakup of the family. Sam has regressed in several ways, including by urinating and defecating in his pants, showing anxiety away from his mother, exhibiting clingy behaviors with his mother, and experiencing nightmares. The youngest child shows some separation anxiety from his mother but generally does fine during day visits with his father.

11. **What is Sam (the oldest child) like? How does his mother describe him? What are her concerns about Sam?**

    Sam is an anxious child. He worries most of the time about his mother and father and the breakup of his family. His anxiety often exhibits as urination or defecation in his pants. He does not like change and needs time to incorporate change into his life. He is struggling right now and is seeing a counselor. He does do well in school, and he has friends.

12. **What is Steve (the youngest child) like? How does his mother describe him? What are her concerns about Steve?**

    Steve is a happy baby. He attends daycare at a licensed child care facility. He is walking and speaking single words. He has good receptive language and understands some sign language.

13. **How does Ann describe Linda (the stepparent)? How do the children get along with Linda?**

    Let's face it—Ann is not a fan of Linda, whom she describes as a woman whose four children all have different fathers. Linda moves herself and her children often and has moved with Bob two times already in their short time living together. Nude pictures of Linda are available on the Internet. Linda also has no functional stepparenting philosophy. She disciplines Sam and allows her 13-year-old daughter to babysit five children while she and Bob go out. She tries to instigate fights with Ann and does drive-bys of Ann's home.

14. **What are Ann's desires for custody and visitation for the children?**

    Ann wants the children to visit their father on alternate weekends from Friday evening to Sunday evening. On the nonweekend visitation weeks, she would like the children to have short evening visits with their father. She wants the visits with Steve to continue to be day visits on alternate Saturdays and Sundays. Holidays can be alternated. Summer visitation would remain the same as during the school year. She also wants Sam to continue to sleep in the upstairs bedroom next to his father's room when he stays overnight with his father.

15. **What are the chances of Ann and Bob becoming reasonable coparents?** It's hard to say at this point without meeting with Bob and Linda. Ann appears to be somewhat dramatic and quite protective of the children but is reasonable and somewhat flexible. She understands the importance of the children's father in their lives.

FATHER'S AND STEPPARENT'S INTERVIEW

The next appointment was with the father, Bob Smith, and his current live-in significant other (referred to as the stepparent), Linda. Their appointment was on January 29, 2010. Bob Smith and Linda came together for their appointment. The interview started with a discussion about the lack of confidentiality in legal cases, what to expect from this interview, and the purpose of the interview. Discussion of money (already done once on the phone when the appointment was set up) and the future appointment with the father and the children took place in more detail at the end of the interview. The evaluator clarified the names and ages of the children, the name of the father's attorney, the name of the mother's attorney, and whether Bob thought Ann was currently living with anyone who was providing stepparenting for the children. All these details were also discussed when the appointment was established.

Bob was also a reasonable person and presented himself well. He spoke clearly and effectively. He was also eager to tell his side of the story. He admitted that he believed that the courts were against him by default because he was a man. There was a discussion about how that might have been true in the past but how, in today's family courts, fathers have the same rights and responsibilities as mothers. The evaluator also discussed the outcome of some previously evaluated cases and how in them the fathers were treated fairly in the court. Bob did not appear to be under the influence of drugs or alcohol. He communicated well and was easy to talk with.

Linda was also dressed appropriately and appeared reasonable. She often spoke for Bob and helped him remember dates of events discussed during the interview. She seemed to be very knowledgeable about Bob's life with Ann, his children, and possible solutions to Bob and Ann's problems. She communicated well but did remain quiet when she was given cues by the evaluator to remain quiet and let Bob talk. Bob and Linda sat close together and often touched each other and held hands during the session.

The following are notes generated during Bob and Linda's interview. The notes will tell much about Bob's perspective on his parenting, Ann's parenting, and their children. The notes also talk about Linda's family and what she brings to this new family. At the end of the interview, Bob paid for his portion of the evaluation and was given a receipt. Discussion of other costs was conducted. An appointment was set up for Bob to bring the children, and the evaluator discussed what to expect during that appointment. Bob was also asked whether he wanted to talk about anything else not already mentioned. The appointment lasted 2 hours:

Father/Stepparent Interview Notes

(continued)

2/

Temp. Order - Current - mid Nov. 2009

diff every wkend
1. dad Thurs 6pm - Sun 6pm every other weekend
dad give day Sat 8-6pm ÷ Sunday 8-6pm
2. Holidays - Thanksgiving - Ann
- Christmas - split
- New Years - Ann

Linda -- children --

girl - Deb - 12 - 7th XXX Jr. High - lives w/ mom
never sees dad - #1
boy - Joe - 11 - 6th XX Elem. - live w/ mom
never sees dad #2
boy - Roy - 8 - 3rd XX Elem. School live w/ dad
sees dad - rarely #3
girl - Beth - 5 - preschool - XXXXX daycare -
sees dad rarely #4

Dad	Mom
3 bedrooms	still in family home
in Lydia neighborhood	no police
no police	no CPA
no CPA	no arrests for Lydia
Linda - arrested child	no D.U.I., DV
enticement - no conviction	
dismissed	

3

Ann has boyfriend Joe –
Ann says they are friends
Joe posts on Facebook bad things
about Bob –
– Joe has DV background x3
– DUI

Sam – 5 – kindergarten –   City Elem. School

< doing good in school –
– has friends at school & XXX daycare
– has problems lying about everything –

goes to csler wkly no alt. wrk – Debbie
dad takes Sam then csler w/ both
Sam & Bob –

wet – pees pants – wears pullups at night
not poops pants

feed himself – picky eater –
personal hygiene
dress himself –

Steve – 19 mos – XXX daycare

happy child

(continued)

4

social child
walking.
crawls upstairs
sleeps in own bed.
sleeps through night
feeds self
good eater
talking — one words —
         — 50% expressive —
         — 100% receptive —
not potty trained —

Desires —

1. 50/50 - wk/wk
         T Th evening visits
   or 4 day rotation —

   or something close to 50/50 —

   Holiday alternate —

Linda doesn't know Ann — seen
her since they live in same neighborhood
Ann went to keep Johaway from his
children
 Like Steve & Sam — Sam spoiled child,
cries often and easily
 Like her children — playful them
he will fit in eventually

He has always been active w/ children
— he would get them up in morning and
feed them
 usually took them to daycare in morning
 and often picked them up at night
— Linda agreed that he was active w/
 his children and her children also
 — she says he's good father

(*continued*)

Relationship w/ Ann OK at beginning –
she became more controlling as
time went on
    She wanted to run marriage and
how children were raised.

Didn't have an affair w/ Linda –
Only friends
    became couple when he moved in
shortly after separation.

    Knew Linda from work – work together –
she is good Mom – good to them
    do family activities together –
    Cheerleading competitions most
every weekend –
        Steve & Sam like to go to them

Denied being alcoholic – drinks but not to
excess – he works – hold management job & couldn't
if he was an alcoholic
    Also denies domestic violence. He doesn't
know why Ann would say those things
No police, no CPS, no arrests

Questions to Consider: Father and Stepparent

Here are some questions to consider after reading the notes generated during Bob and Linda's interview. Remember: These do not tell the entire story—just Bob's side of it.

1. What, in Bob's perspective, was the family like prior to the breakup?
2. How would you describe the relationship Ann and Bob had during their marriage?
3. Who was the primary caregiver during the marriage?
4. Were alcohol or drugs a problem in the marriage?
5. Was either parent unfaithful during the marriage?
6. Why did they separate?
7. What were the arrangements for visitation after the separation?
8. Where are the parents currently living?
9. Are there any temporary visitation orders in place?
10. Are the temporary orders working for the children?
11. What is Sam (the oldest child) like? How does his father describe him? What are his concerns about Sam?
12. What is Steve (the youngest child) like? How does his father describe him? What are his concerns about Steve?
13. How does Linda describe Ann? How well does she get along with Ann?
14. What are Bob's desires for custody and visitation for the children?
15. What are the chances of Ann and Bob becoming reasonable coparents?
16. How do the children relate to Linda?
17. What is Linda's stepparenting philosophy?
18. Do Bob and Linda have reasonable expectations for a successful blended family?
19. Between Bob and Linda, who provides most of the parenting when the children are at Bob's house?
20. What is the relationship like between Bob and Linda?

Now let's compare your answers with those of the evaluator. You are getting the idea that there are always two sides to the story—and that they are generally different in high-conflict cases. Never make your mind up about your recommendations until you hear all sides and gather enough information to validate the recommendations you do make.

Questions to Consider: Father and Stepparent/ Evaluator's Answers

1. **What, in Bob's perspective, was the family like prior to the breakup?**
   The notes do a fairly good job detailing what Bob thought about the marriage before the breakup. He thought Ann was controlling and would try to

run the family. They got along all right, but he had a great deal of responsibility for child care in the family. He fed the children breakfast each morning and took them to daycare. He often put them to bed at night. He described himself as a hands-on father. He grew tired of Ann's constant nagging and talked to Linda about his marriage. He denied having an affair with Linda—he says that they weren't intimate until they began living together.

2. **How would you describe the relationship Ann and Bob had during their marriage?**

   Bob denied being an alcoholic, though he said he drank a few drinks occasionally. He described Ann as being overly dramatic when it came to his drinking. He denied ever hitting her or breaking anything when he was drinking. There are no police reports or arrests pertaining to the alleged domestic violence. Bob said the marriage started out good but went downhill after Sam was born: He and Ann grew apart.

3. **Who was the primary caregiver during the marriage?**

   Bob suggested that he was the primary caregiver, but the evaluator didn't buy his argument for that role. However, he was involved in parenting the children.

4. **Were alcohol or drugs a problem in the marriage?**

   Bob denies that drugs or alcohol were ever an issue in the marriage. He has no arrests or DUIs, and no police reports recording calls to the home for domestic violence.

5. **Was either parent unfaithful during the marriage?**

   Bob said he was not unfaithful during the marriage. He moved in with Linda soon after leaving the marriage, but he wasn't "with" Linda until they began living together. Bob is concerned about Ann's current boyfriend, who has a recorded DUI and a background of domestic violence. He also speaks maliciously about Bob on Facebook.

6. **Why did they separate?**

   Bob's reason for the separation had nothing to do with domestic violence, alcoholism, or infidelity. He just didn't want to be with Ann anymore.

7. **What were the arrangements for visitation after the separation?**

   He generally agreed with what Ann said about the visitation arrangements after the separation. He did say that he took the children to Linda's house and didn't return them to Ann when she requested. He said that he didn't have to do what Ann told him to do—they were his children, too. Things have gotten better since the temporary order, because now he and Ann can't fight about who has the children and for how long.

8. **Where are the parents currently living?**

   Ann is currently living in the family home, and Bob is living with Linda and her four children in a home they rent. He did acknowledge that they have moved two times but said that they are now situated in a home that is large enough for all the children and that is located in the same neighborhood as the original family home.

9. Are there any temporary visitation orders in place?
   Yes, and the parents agree on what the orders say.
10. Are the temporary orders working for the children?
    Bob thinks they are, but he thinks they could be improved by allowing the children to spend more time with him. He also wants overnights with his youngest son.
11. What is Sam (the oldest child) like? How does his father describe him? What are his concerns about Sam?
    Bob describes Sam as doing well in school and having friends. He also says that Sam lies about everything and thus can't be believed when he tells stories. Bob agrees that Sam urinates in his pants but says he doesn't defecate in them. Bob says that Sam is a picky eater and a picky child. Sam worries a lot about things and doesn't like changes in his routine.
12. What is Steve (the youngest child) like? How does his father describe him? What are his concerns about Steve?
    Bob describes Steve as a happy child. He is walking and sleeps in his own bed through the night. He can crawl up stairsteps. He can feed himself. He talks in single words and has good receptive language.
13. How does Linda describe Ann? How well does she get along with Ann?
    Linda thinks Ann is jealous of the relationship that she and Bob share. She really doesn't know Ann and doesn't want to know her. She thinks Ann is hypervigilant about the children.
14. What are Bob's desires for custody and visitation for the children?
    Bob wants both children for half the time. He would like a week/week rotation but would consider a 4-day rotation. He also wants evening visits with the children on the weeks when Ann has the children. Holidays could be alternated.
15. What are the chances of Ann and Bob becoming reasonable coparents?
    The jury is still out on that question. Bob does not really want to communicate with Ann. He does not like her to tell him what to do when it comes to his time with the children. However, he is able to talk with her effectively on occasion.
16. How do the children relate to Linda?
    Linda describes everything as being fine when the children are with her and Bob. She gets along well with Bob's children, and they get along great with her children.
17. What is Linda's stepparenting philosophy?
    She treats them like her own children. She doesn't show favoritism to any of the children. She is very involved in her older children's extracurricular activities. The family attends these children's competitions almost every weekend.
18. Do Bob and Linda have reasonable expectations for a successful blended family?
    They describe what they think is already a successful blended family.

19. **Between Bob and Linda, who provides most of the parenting when the children are at Bob's house?**
    Linda provides most of the parenting, but Bob is also actively involved. Linda works a late shift, so Bob is responsible for the children in the evenings and before bedtime. He also attends Linda's children's weekend competitions. He is trying to balance his life with six children and a new relationship.

20. **What is the relationship like between Bob and Linda?**
    It appears that Bob and Linda have a committed relationship to each other now. Statistically, such relationships do not generally succeed, but for now it appears that Bob and Linda are committed to each other. Linda orchestrates the family, including what Bob is expected to do in it. Linda is protective of Bob, as he is of her.

REVIEW OF INFORMATION GATHERED FROM PARENT INTERVIEWS

Now that the evaluator has met with both parents, let's compile what we know, what we don't know, and what we want to verify with other contacts. There is still a long way to go before you write the recommendations, but the picture is beginning to become more detailed.

What we know is that both parents seem to be reasonable people. They disagree on what would work best for the children when it comes to custody and visitation, but they appear to both love the children very much and want what is best for them. We also know that neither parent communicates well with the other parent nor particularly wants to talk with the other parent. Ann is likely to coparent more effectively than Bob, at least in the beginning. Both parents describe the children similarly, especially Steve. They do agree that Sam is an anxious child, doesn't handle change well, does well in school, and has friends. They both agree that he is struggling with the breakup of the family.

What they disagree on is the role of Bob's drinking in the ultimate demise of the family. Ann talked at length about Bob's alcoholism; Bob denied there was any problem. Ann talked about the domestic violence that occurred in the marriage; Bob denied there was ever domestic violence. Ann reported that Bob was controlling; Bob claimed Ann was bossy and controlling. Ann thinks that Bob was having an affair with Linda prior to the breakup of the marriage; Bob says this is untrue. They do not agree on Sam's regression: Ann says Sam urinates and defecates in his pants; Bob says Sam only urinates in his pants. Ann says Sam doesn't get along with Linda and her children. Bob insists that Sam and Steve get along very well with Linda and her children.

What we still don't know is whether the drinking and domestic violence should play a significant role in the recommendations: There have been no arrests or police involvement. It really is her word against his. Bob also says that Sam is a liar and tells stories that are not true, though Ann did not describe her son that way.

The evaluator will have access to the report that was written previously about this case, and that may or may not clarify some of these unknowns. We also don't know how Sam relates to Linda and her children. The parents describe his interactions differently. We also don't know what role, if any, Linda plays in keeping these parents from coparenting effectively. Finally, we haven't discovered how long the relationship between Bob and Linda will last. They insist that this relationship is the real thing—but it is a rebound relationship for Bob. Additionally, Bob says that he left his marriage with Ann because she was too controlling, but Linda seems as controlling as Bob claims Ann was, if not more so. There is still much to be learned before any recommendations can be reached.

MOTHER'S AND CHILDREN'S INTERVIEW

The next appointment was with Ann and the children, Sam (age 5, kindergarten) and Steve (age 19 months). Ann brought the children in about a week after her appointment. As previously discussed, Ann and the children worked together on a project while the evaluator observed them. The task was to build a collage of things that remind Sam of things he likes or has done with his mother or father. Steve was too young to engage in the task but remained in the room, and his mother was responsible for keeping him entertained and engaged while also dealing with Sam.

At the beginning of the session, the evaluator introduced herself briefly to Sam and Steve and then took Ann and the children to a room containing a stack of magazines, large pieces of blank paper, markers, colored pencils, several pairs of scissors (both children's and adult), tape, and glue sticks. Instructions were given to Ann and the children, and they began the task. The evaluator sat off to the side observing the interactions between Ann and the children. This portion of the appointment lasted approximately 40 minutes. Notifications about time were given at 5 minutes, 3 minutes, and 1 minute.

The following are the notes from the observation of the task with Ann and the children:

Mother's and Children's Interview Notes

1-30-10 — Ann and Children
Sam - 5 - Kind
Steve - 19 mos.

Steve - bit fussy - just woke up from nap
Clingy to mom
did finally warm up to me -
smiled at me
interited in mag. pictures and
what his mother was doing
- liked holding colored pens
- sat on mom's lap

Sam - easily engaged in colage task
- verbal - easily understood
- really liked using tape dispenser
- conversation w/ mom on-going -
mom attentive
- compliant to mom's requests
- gave mom orders -

Steve communicated w/ mom? Sam)
Sam helped Steve get a piece of tape -

Sam had fairly good scissor skills -
found lots of pictures

> 2
>
> Worked mostly indep. of mom
>
> Steve & Sam worked together getting tape for colage - mom helped also
>
> Mom had easy relationship w/ both boys - easily handled both boys and their needs -

Questions to Consider: Mother and Children

1. Was Ann able to control both children during the activity? Was she able to keep them engaged in appropriate behaviors?
2. Did Sam engage in the activity?
3. What were the interactions between Ann and Sam during the activity?
4. What were the interactions between Ann and Steve during the activity?
5. What were the interactions between Sam and Steve during the activity?
6. How would you describe the relationship that Sam had with his mother?
7. How would you describe the relationship that Steve had with his mother?
8. How would you describe the relationship that Sam and Steve had with each other?
9. What was the feeling in the room when they were working on the activity?
10. What do you know about Sam and Steve from your observations?

Now see whether your responses to the questions matched the thinking of the evaluator. Remember: The evaluator had the advantage of doing the actual observation, so your responses may be different depending on the quality of the evaluator's notes. However, your responses should be at least close to the evaluator's.

Questions to Consider: Mother and Children/
Evaluator's Answers

1. **Was Ann able to control both children during the activity? Was she able to keep them engaged in appropriate behaviors?**

   Ann easily handled the two children. Steve started out a bit fussy, having just awakened from a nap, but he warmed up as time went on. Sam was compliant with his mother's requests and was engaged in the activity, as was Steve (for his developmental level).

2. **Did Sam engage in the activity?**

   Sam was very engaged in the activity. He found many pictures, liked taping them on the paper, and seemed to enjoy the creativity of the task. He talked throughout the activity to both his mother and his brother.

3. **What were the interactions between Ann and Sam during the activity?**

   Ann and Sam talked with each other throughout the activity. Their conversation was easy and flowed well. Sam was compliant with his mother's requests. He also felt comfortable enough with his mother to give her instructions. Ann was compliant with his requests and was very attentive to him and to his words and actions. Ann had an easy relationship with Sam.

4. **What were the interactions between Ann and Steve during the activity?**

   Ann and Steve interacted with each other appropriately. At first Steve clung to Ann and sat on her lap. As time went on, he sat in his own chair and participated in the activity to the extent of his ability. Ann responded to Steve's requests, encouraging him and praising him appropriately. Ann had an easy relationship with Steve.

5. **What were the interactions between Sam and Steve during the activity?**

   Sam and Steve interacted with each other: Sam helped his brother get tape, gave him colored pencils to hold, and talked to him. Sam seemed to understand what Steve wanted and was compliant with his requests. The boys had an easy relationship with each other.

6. **How would you describe the relationship that Sam had with his mother?**

   The relationship was functional, loving, and comfortable. Sam related to his mother very easily. He engaged her in conversation and engaged with her in performing the task. Everyone helped everyone else. Sam loves his mother very much, and she loves him.

7. **How would you describe the relationship that Steve had with his mother?**

   Steve had a loving and comfortable relationship with his mother. He looked for her to comfort him when he was fussy and looked to her for assistance with the tape and for attention when he needed it. They engaged in conversation. Steve was happy to be there with his mother and his brother. Steve loves his mother very much, and she loves him.

8. **How would you describe the relationship that Sam and Steve had with each other?**

   Sam and Steve interacted easily with each other during the task. Sam was helpful to his brother and was compliant with his requests. They shared well, didn't grab objects out of each others' hands, and got along well with each other. Sam was protective of Steve. He appears to take his job of big brother seriously.

9. **What was the feeling in the room when they were working on the activity?**
The feeling was a good one. There was no tension or anxiety. Everyone got along with everyone. There was humor in the conversations. Both boys and Ann were relaxed and enjoyed the task.

10. **What do you know about Sam and Steve from your observations?**
Sam and Steve are bonded with each other, as they also are with their mother. Sam is a nice boy and feels comfortable with his mother. He is protective of his brother and his mother. He tries hard to please and do a good job. He is meticulous in his work. Sam is developmentally appropriate with his language and motor skills. He is a nice boy and would be easy for a counselor to work with. Steve is also developmentally appropriate for his age. He is curious and acts independently in his environment. He has excellent receptive language and appropriate expressive language skills and is confident that both his mother and Sam will understand what he needs and will provide for him. He is a nice boy and is developing positively.

CHILD INTERVIEW

After this part of the appointment, Ann and Steve were asked to leave the room, and the evaluator and Sam spent some time together one on one. This part of the appointment lasted approximately 40 minutes. Sam was not reluctant to stay alone with the evaluator and engaged in conversation easily. He seemed comfortable and interacted with the evaluator appropriately.

The evaluator began by asking about the collage Sam had made, talking about the pictures and why Sam chose those particular ones. The evaluator then told him what she knew about him, including his grade in school, that he did well in school, and that he had friends (she asked about their names). Then she tried to guess Sam's favorite subject in school. She guessed correctly after two tries. Sam was impressed with the evaluator's skills (as are virtually all children). Sam was easy to develop rapport with and was willing to talk openly with the evaluator. Sam was a really nice boy to be around.

The evaluator asked Sam whether he knew why he was there talking to the evaluator. He said that it was because his mother and father fought and couldn't get along with each other. The evaluator agreed and told him that because his mother and father couldn't get along well enough to decide how they would both see the children, they hired the evaluator to help them make decisions; because Sam was part of the family, the evaluator wanted to talk with him to hear what he thought of the situation and find out whether he had any ideas about how to make his life easier. Sam thought this was a good idea. The evaluator told Sam that she was working for him, so he was the boss and the evaluator his employee. Sam really liked that idea.

The following notes were written by the evaluator after the appointment with Sam:

Child Interview Notes

Same w/ me –

Doesn't like it at dad's house.
Better now that he got to move upstairs
in Steve's room. Afraid in the basement
likes Deb, Joe & Beth a ____ – Roy
mean to him – hits him gets him in trouble
Doesn't like Linda ____ she doesn't like him
either – she puts in time out, yells at him –
takes Roy's side over him
4 days w/ mom too short
3 days w/ dad too long – wants one day
with day.
Misses mom when w/ dad

Primary Care giver – MOM
1st thing he told me was that he saw dad hurting
mom – wouldn't talk about it anymore

Sam began to talk immediately about how much he hates being at his father's house. At first, he had to sleep in a room in the basement, and that scared him. His father finally moved him into a room upstairs next to his own room, which they had reserved for Steve. Sam likes that better and doesn't feel as afraid.

Sam gets along with three of Linda's four children, but the 8-year-old boy, Roy, is always mean to Sam and gets him into trouble all the time. Sam also doesn't like Linda: She makes him eat food he doesn't like and always sides with Roy against him. She likes her children, but she doesn't like Sam. She wants everyone to only do the things her children want to do.

Sam misses his mother when he is at his father's. He believes 4 days with his mother to be too few and 3 days with his father to be too many. He worries about his mother and Steve when he is not with them. He is afraid that his father won't let him leave with his mother when it is time for him to go to her house. He feels afraid and sad and mad when he is at his father's.

Sam told the evaluator that he once saw his father hurt his mother. He said so first thing and then didn't want to talk about it anymore. The comment was odd in happening first, as if Sam wanted to get it out of the way. Sam agreed that he was scared when it happened, then moved on to other topics. The evaluator wonders whether he was coached by his mother or whether he thought this was what he was supposed to talk about based on his prior experience with an evaluator. Further thought is needed on this topic and Sam's involvement.

Here are some questions to consider regarding the interview with Sam:

Questions to Consider: Child

1. Who does Sam view as his primary caregiver?
2. What is Sam's experience at his mother's house?
3. What is Sam's experience at his father's house?
4. How does Sam relate to Linda's children?
5. How does Sam relate to Linda?
6. What does Sam want for a custody and visitation schedule?

Questions to Consider: Child/ Evaluator's Answers

1. **Who does Sam view as his primary caregiver?**
   Sam views his mother as his primary caregiver. Steve is too young to speak, but he is certainly bonded with his mother.
2. **What is Sam's experience at his mother's house?**
   Sam feels comfortable and safe at his mother's house. He doesn't like change in his life. At his mother's home—the family home—he is in familiar surroundings and has all his things.
3. **What is Sam's experience at his father's house?**
   Sam feels uncomfortable, worried, anxious, and afraid at his father's house. He is picked on by the other children and often gets in trouble. He believes that Linda sides with her children and doesn't like him. When he is at his father's house, he worries about his mother and brother.
4. **How does Sam relate to Linda's children?**
   He gets along with three of the four children, but Roy, the 8-year-old, picks on him and gets him into trouble. He feels left out and unliked by the other children.
5. **How does Sam relate to Linda?**
   He believes that she doesn't like him and that she treats him differently from how she treats her own children. She is mean to him. She also makes his father do what she wants him to do rather than letting him spend time with Sam.
6. **What does Sam want for a custody and visitation schedule?**
   Sam wants more time with his mother and less time with his father. He misses his mother when he is at his father's house—he wants to go home. He is afraid that his father won't let him leave with his mother when it is time for Sam to go with her.

FATHER AND CHILDREN INTERVIEW

The last appointment was with Bob and the children, approximately 2 weeks after Bob and Linda's appointment. Sam remembered the evaluator and showed Bob to the room where Sam and Steve had worked previously with their mother. Sam was eager to begin the collage activity with his father. The evaluator asked whether Sam could give his father instructions, which he did; then they began the activity. Steve was also interested in what was going on and wanted to play with the tape. Bob had brought food and drink for Steve to eat since it was close to lunchtime. This portion of the appointment lasted approximately 40 minutes.

After considering the notes taken during this portion of the appointment, see whether you can answer the following questions:

Father and Children Interview Notes

2-11-10   Both Children
            Sam - 5 - kind
            Steve - 19 months

Sam easily engaged in task of Colage
" told dad how to do colage;
how to tape -

dad brought Steve Cheerios to eat
" a drink - he was content to
set and eat " drink
            fed himself
            sippy cup
            entertained himself while sitting in chair
dad actively involved w/ ___ and'd
            building colage
            - Sam compleant w/ his requests
            - Sam gave him orders
            - gave Sam "choices, helped w/ scissors
polite" w/ each other

Sam still has scissor trouble sometimes
but did better with taping

Steve - good eye contact w/ dad / w/ me
            - smiled w/ dad / w/ me

(continued)

2.

"Talked" to dad - recognized him
"daddy"
- good relationship w/ dad

Steve had easy rel w/ dad also

dad very patient w/ Steve helping dad
draw - Steve held on to top of pen
while dad drew

Appropriate encouragement/praise for
- both boys -

Questions to Consider:
Father and Children

1. Was Bob able to control both children during the activity? Was he able to keep them engaged in appropriate behaviors?
2. Did Sam engage in the activity?
3. What were the interactions between Bob and Sam during the activity?
4. What were the interactions between Bob and Steve during the activity?
5. What were the interactions between Sam and Steve during the activity?
6. How would you describe the relationship that Sam had with his father?
7. How would you describe the relationship that Steve had with his father?
8. How would you describe the relationship that Sam and Steve had with each other?
9. What was the feeling in the room when they were working on the activity?
10. What do you know about Sam and Steve from your observations?

Questions to Consider: Father and Children/
Evaluator's Answers

Here are the evaluator's thoughts about the questions. Now that you are getting the hang of this, your answers are probably similar.

1. **Was Bob able to control both children during the activity? Was he able to keep them engaged in appropriate behaviors?**
   Bob was able to handle both children during the activity. He kept them both engaged in the activity. He showed patience in his interactions with both Sam and Steve. He encouraged and praised them both appropriately.
2. **Did Sam engage in the activity?**
   Yes, Sam engaged in the activity and encouraged his father to be an active participant as well.
3. **What were the interactions between Bob and Sam during the activity?**
   Bob and Sam talked throughout the activity. Sam was compliant with his father's requests and felt comfortable enough to give his father instructions. His father was compliant with Sam's requests. They had fun together and conversed with each other easily.
4. **What were the interactions between Bob and Steve during the activity?**
   Bob and Steve interacted well together. Bob helped him draw and participate. Bob was very patient with Steve, giving him appropriate praise and encouragement.
5. **What were the interactions between Sam and Steve during the activity?**
   Again, Sam helped Steve with the tape. Sam waited for his father's attention when Bob was dealing with Steve. Sam talked to Steve often during the activity.
6. **How would you describe the relationship that Sam had with his father?**
   Sam and his father have a good relationship with each other. They appear bonded and easily interact with each other. They use humor with each other and have an easy relationship.
7. **How would you describe the relationship that Steve had with his father?**
   Steve also appeared bonded with his father. He had good eye contact with his father. He depended on his father to fulfill his requests. He smiled a lot at both Sam and his father.
8. **How would you describe the relationship that Sam and Steve had with each other?**
   The relationship between Sam and Steve was similar to what happened during the appointment with Ann. They related well with each other. Sam was willing to help Steve participate in the activity. Both boys shared well with each other.
9. **What was the feeling in the room when they were working on the activity?**
   There was a good feeling in the room during the activity. Everyone got along and seemed happy to be with each other. There was a sense of a solid relationship between the boys and their father.
10. **What do you know about Sam and Steve from your observations?**
    Both of the boys are good children and easy to be around. The evaluator drew the same conclusions about the boys during this appointment that she did from the appointment with their mother.

This activity showed the evaluator that the boys had a good relationship with their father. He was attentive to both children's needs. He paid appropriate attention to both boys. Bob engaged in conversation with both children and used humor with both boys. He listened to the children when they wanted his attention. Bob demonstrated that he had the patience to deal with the boys and that he had built a firm relationship with both children.

CHILD INTERVIEW

As before, Bob and Steve were asked to leave the room. Sam was fine with staying alone with the evaluator, who started by talking about the collage Sam had built with his father. Then Sam talked about what he and his father were going to do together that day. He was very happy that he and Steve and their father were going to spend the day alone together. He wished that his father would spend more time alone with him. He was happy when he was with his father and unhappy when his father spent most of his time with Linda and her children.

Here are the notes from this portion of the appointment. Read them and then answer the following questions:

Child Interview Notes

Sam w/ me —

Very verbal
dev. appropriate
advanced writing/reading skills

drew his family   Sam dad, step mom grandma
                                              grandpa
                                   uncle x44 &
                                     cousin#1
                                    cousin#2
                                    cousin#3
                                    evaluator

still wanted more time w/ mom
less w/ dad
finally just ignored talk about

3

mom dad he was having fun drawing
on board

Questions to Consider: Child

1. Who does Sam view as his primary caregiver?
2. What is Sam's experience at his mother's house?
3. What is Sam's experience at his father's house?
4. How does Sam relate to Linda's children?
5. How does Sam relate to Linda?
6. What does Sam want for a custody and visitation schedule?

Questions to Consider: Child/ Evaluator's Answers

Here are the evaluator's answers:

1. **Who does Sam view as his primary caregiver?**
   Sam remains consistent in viewing his mother as the primary caregiver.
2. **What is Sam's experience at his mother's house?**
   Again, he remains consistent in feeling most comfortable at his mother's house.
3. **What is Sam's experience at his father's house?**
   Sam didn't change his opinion about being at his father's house from the first time the evaluator talked with him.
4. **How does Sam relate to Linda's children?**
   This, too, remains consistent from the first interview.
5. **How does Sam relate to Linda?**
   Again, there is no new information about his feelings toward Linda. Nothing has changed since the first discussion with the evaluator.
6. **What does Sam want for a custody and visitation schedule?**
   Sam still wants more time with his mother and less time at his father's house.

Sam remained consistent in wanting more time with his mother and less time at his father's house. He still didn't like it at his father's house—he didn't like Linda, and he didn't like her children. His feelings remained consistent about his father's house and his mother's house. He said he had thought about the previous one-on-one discussion and still wanted his family together, but if that couldn't happen then he wanted to spend his time with his mother and spend alone time with his father. But he didn't think that alone time with his father was going to happen, because Linda wanted his father to do things with her and her children.

Then, as often happens, Sam was done talking about his mother and his father. He began to draw on the board. He drew his family, including his parents, his brother, his grandparents, his uncle, and his cousins. He also included the evaluator at the end of the line of people. He did not include Linda or her children.

He talked about how he plays with his cousins and his friends. He enjoyed drawing on the board while talking about what he likes to do for fun. Although Bob and Linda agreed that Sam liked to go to Linda's children's competitions, Sam did not mention doing that as something that he enjoyed doing.

Now you have a feeling for the children and the parents. You understand how each home operates and how the children fit into each home. You also understand how successful the blending of the two families at Bob's home is both from Bob's perspective and from Sam's perspective. You know what the relationships are like between the children and each parent. You also know what Sam wants in order for his life to be better, what the parents want in terms of custody and visitation, and what might meet the best interests of the children.

COLLATERAL CONTACTS

Next is the information gathered from the collateral contacts and the collateral documents. Let's start with the collateral contacts, including Sam's current counselor and both the children's daycare providers. The first notes are those taken when the evaluator talked with Sam's counselor on the telephone:

Collateral Contacts:
Child's Counselor Notes

2-14-10 — Debbie XXX — XXXX— Csling Center

seen Oct. 3
Came weekly now alt wk
out going
cooperative
appropriate child
typically doesn't have concerns about
mom — concerns about stepchildren

good rel w/ dad
good rel. w/ mom

worrier — doesn't like changes
easy target for step children picking on him
w/o other children in house maybe more
time but not the way it is now
he's not ready for shared arrangement
really doesn't like change - doesn't like
it at dad's house
likes being w/ dad but not
other children
better when moved upstairs near dad's room to sleep
no concerns about mom's parenting —
communicative, responsive

No mention of DV in sessions

Questions to Consider: Collateral Contact—Child Counselor

Now that you have read the notes, answer the following questions:

1. Do Sam and the counselor have a good therapeutic relationship?
2. Is the counselor's interpretation of Sam similar to what you have concluded?
3. What is the counselor's perspective of both parents and of Sam's relationship with them?
4. Did the counselor have any concerns about either parent's skills as a parent to Sam?
5. Did the counselor have an opinion about what custody and visitation schedule would work best for Sam?

Questions to Consider: Collateral Contact—Child Counselor/Evaluator's Answers

Here's how the evaluator answered these questions.

1. Do Sam and the counselor have a good therapeutic relationship?
   Yes, Sam and his counselor do have a good therapeutic relationship. They have engaged in counseling for more than 3 months. He is a cooperative and appropriate child in therapy.
2. Is the counselor's interpretation of Sam similar to what you have concluded?
   Yes, the counselor describes Sam the way the evaluator sees him. He is a nice boy but struggles with change. He is anxious and a worrier. He doesn't like it at his father's house. He doesn't get along with Linda's children. He is an easy target for the other children to pick on.
3. What is the counselor's perspective of both parents and of Sam's relationship with them?
   The counselor describes both parents as having good parenting abilities. She has had more contact with Ann but believes that Sam has a good relationship with both his parents. He likes spending time with both his parents. He wants more time alone with his father without the other children or Linda around.
4. Did the counselor have any concerns about either parent's skills as a parent to Sam?
   No, she didn't have any concerns about the parents' abilities to parent Sam. She did worry that Bob is not spending quality time with Sam.
5. Did the counselor have an opinion about what custody and visitation schedule would work best for Sam?
   Yes, she was opposed to a shared arrangement at this time. She thought that more time with Bob would be fine so long as Linda's children were not present. She believed that Ann was the primary caregiver for the children.

One area of interest was that, according to the counselor, Sam had never mentioned the domestic violence that he told the evaluator he had observed. It is interesting that Sam would not talk about this in therapy. He did openly talk about his troubles fitting into Bob's new family. He discussed missing his mother when he was at his father's house. He also talked about worrying about his mother and brother when he was not with them. He wants to spend time with his father, but not with the other children or Linda. He felt as if his father was doing more for Linda and her children than for Sam or Steve.

The next collateral contacts were the children's daycare providers. Both conversations were relatively short but revealed important information. After reading the notes, answer the following questions:

Collateral Contacts: Daycare Providers' Notes

```
2-14-10- Susan -. XXX daycare center
Steve - almost 1 year -
developmental appropriate
good receptive language
Steve happy to go w/ either parent
really happy boy -
not neglected
no concerns about either parent
- only met dad a few times - most
contact is w/ mom


Jane -XXX daycare left msg X2
```

(continued)

2-15-10   Jane - XXX daycare Center

Sam daycare provider ≈ 1 1/2 years

Sam is good boy - basically happy boy
he is anxious and does worry

mom is more involved w/ him at daycare
- he is clingy to her
dad is OK too - Sam goes easily w/ him

since breakup Sam has had more accidents
- pee & poop
Views mom as primary care giver

Questions to Consider: Collateral
Contact—Daycare Providers

1. Are the children well cared for, or do they appear neglected?
2. Do the children have a good relationship with both parents?
3. Do the children act appropriately at daycare?
4. Have there been any noticeable changes in either child since the breakup of the family?

Questions to Consider: Collateral
Contact—Daycare Providers/Evaluator's Answers

Here is how the evaluator answered the questions; your answers should be similar.

1. **Are the children well cared for, or do they appear neglected?**
   Both children are well cared for and do not seem neglected. They are clean, well-fed, happy children.
2. **Do the children have a good relationship with both parents?**
   Yes, they seem to have a good relationship with both parents. Both child care providers had more contact with Ann (contrary to what Bob said in his interview). The children go with either parent willingly when picked up.

3. **Do the children act appropriately at daycare?**
   Yes. They are good children and do not cause disruption at the daycare facility. They both appear to be developmentally appropriate.
4. **Have there been any noticeable changes in either child since the breakup of the family?**
   Sam has had more accidents since the breakup of the family. He both urinates and defecates in his pants more often. This is a change in his behavior. He also appears to be more anxious and worried since the breakup.

Collateral Contacts: Documentation

Now let's consider the documentation that was submitted to the evaluator to consider. First, let's start with the mini-evaluation that was completed approximately 3 months before the full evaluation was ordered. The purpose of this evaluation was to give recommendations for temporary custody and visitation. It was hoped that the mini-evaluation would resolve the problems between the parents so that they could then develop a parenting plan without further involvement from the court.

Collateral Contact: Prior Evaluation

The prior mini-evaluation was 14 pages long and contained details about the parents, the children, and the parents' respective homes. It also gave recommendations for custody and visitation. Unfortunately, numerous problems with the report and its recommendations did little to help the full evaluation process.

   This mini-evaluation included discussion of both parents' skills and relationships with the children. It also included the role of Linda in Bob's home. The evaluator stated in the report that she had met with both parents, with both children, and with both parents together with their children and that she had made telephone contacts with the collateral contacts provided by each parent, in addition to making in-home visits. The inaccuracies in the report start at its beginning: This evaluator did not get the timeline correct after Bob moved out of the family home. Next, the report dwelled on both parents' accusations of the other's infidelities before the separation. This was questionable—what an evaluator needs to deal with is the reality of the present situation of the children and their parents.

   The report discusses at length in-home visits to the mother's home. The evaluator verified that there were broken doors and holes in walls and had Sam show her where his father used to keep his beer in the garage. She also talked privately to Sam twice in his mother's home. These interviews focused on having Sam tell her about the domestic violence he had observed between his mother and father. The evaluator also had Sam discuss living at his father's home and how he hated it and felt scared there. He also talked about how Linda treated him and the other children and said that he didn't like her or like being at his father's house. The evaluator asked Sam to tell her about how Steve was treated at Bob's home by Linda. Bob later called these interviews interrogations. Perhaps it was just how these conversations were written—but they did sound a bit like interrogations of Sam.

The report then goes on to tell how Bob tried to intimidate the evaluator into giving him shared custody of the children. The evaluator said she later received a call from Bob apologizing for making her feel as if he was intimidating her. The evaluator apparently did not believe the apology was heartfelt—the report listed this as a continued cause for concern during the evaluation. Did events happen as the evaluator described, or was the evaluator too sensitive? This will remain unknown.

The report details the evaluator's in-home visits in both parents' homes. It was later revealed that the visits in Ann's home were quite exhaustive, but the visit at Bob's home was not. The evaluator went through the entire house and garage at Ann's but simply sat on the couch in one room at Bob's. She then developed her conclusions despite the inequities in her visits. This is never a good idea. What the evaluator does for one parent he or she should replicate for the other.

Before providing recommendations, the report described the evaluator's collateral contacts. However, Bob's contacts were not contacted by the evaluator. Furthermore, the report says that the evaluator saw the children with both their parents. This, too, was untrue—she only saw the children with their mother.

The lessons to learn from this report are numerous. If you didn't contact someone, then don't say you did. Also, treat both parents fairly—and equally. Do not write a report that seems to favor one parent over the other. Treat both parents the same. Additionally, do not perseverate on one aspect of the situation. The evaluator was determined to make Sam and Ann's allegations of domestic violence a major factor in her recommendations to the court. But many factors must play into reasonable recommendations. Finally, your recommendations must make sense and be consistent with your previous discussion in the report. If the evaluator writes that Bob is prone to domestic violence, then the recommendations should reflect how the children will be protected when they are with him. Consider whether this evaluation's recommendations do that.

The recommendations given to the court by the mini-evaluation were for longer than the 3-month temporary custody and visitation schedule required by this type of evaluation. The recommendations for the best interest of the children included a week/week shared arrangement for both children during the summer months. Also included was a 2-week extended vacation period for Bob during the summer. If Bob was prone to violence, Linda a poor stepparent, and Sam not fitting in with Linda's children and feeling troubled about being at his father's home for long periods, then why would a shared arrangement be in Sam's best interest? Steve is far too young to be away from his primary caregiver and his primary home. A week away (and 2 weeks on one occasion) from his mother is far from being in his best interests.

During the school year, it was recommended that the children visit their father on alternate weekends from Friday evening to Sunday evening. Again, this is not reasonable for a child of Steve's age. It does make more sense for Sam and his best interest. A holiday schedule for the entire year was also included.

Further recommendations include parenting classes for both parents. That is not a bad idea—but what about classes for the person who was described as needing them the most—Linda? Anger management classes, alcohol awareness classes, and domestic violence classes were also recommended for Bob. Both parents were recommended to engage in counseling with Sam together and then with Linda and Sam together. This was not a good recommendation. Putting all the adults in a room together has the potential for being a catastrophe for everyone involved. Remember: This is a high-conflict case. Finally, it was recommended that the parents undergo mediation to resolve any other problems in developing a parenting plan.

Ultimately, Bob and his attorney requested that the court exclude this report and order a full evaluation with another evaluator agreed upon by both parents. The attorney provided the court with affidavits from those people not contacted and an affidavit from Bob stating he that was not involved with the children during the evaluation, as well as with other pieces of evidence that in aggregate persuaded the court to exclude the report.

Collateral Contact: Prior Evaluation/ Evaluator's Answers

In regard to the current evaluation, the first mini-evaluation was not particularly helpful except in verifying the consistency in which Sam spoke of his father's home, his feelings about being at his father's house, his feelings about and experiences with Linda and her children, and his mother's being his primary caregiver. These issues could have been discovered without reading the first mini-evaluation.

Collateral Contact: Father's Deposition

Another document provided to the evaluator was the deposition of Bob taken prior to the order of the current evaluation. This 57-page document provided little, if no, additional information relevant to the children's best interests. Finally, Ann provided nude pictures of Linda she acquired on the Internet. She provided other pictures, also available on the Internet, showing Linda, Bob, Linda's children, and Bob's children as one big happy family. Again, neither of these collateral pieces provided information particularly relevant to the children's best interests.

EVALUATOR'S CONSIDERATIONS FOR RECOMMENDATIONS

Now it is the job of the evaluator to decide what information is important to writing appropriate recommendations and what information is irrelevant to the primary purpose. Four main pieces of information that will provide a map to writing the recommendations are: (1) Steve's age; (2) Sam's feelings about his father's house, particularly Linda and her children; Sam's regression, evident in his return to urinating and defecating in his pants; Sam's constant worry about what will happen to him, his brother, and his mother; and Sam's inability to cope with change and stress; (3) Ann's role as the primary caregiver for the children; and (4) both children's good relationship with both their parents.

The other information, including Bob's alcohol use and alleged domestic violence, infidelity on one or both parents' parts, Linda's past with men and subsequent four children, availability of nude pictures of Linda on the Internet, and Linda's apparent lack of understanding of the role of a stepparent, are certainly part of this case, but they are not the driving forces behind your recommendations to the court. You may find some of these things offensive, but your job is to write recommendations that are in the children's best interest, nothing more.

The following are the recommendations the evaluator provided to the court. You should be able to understand how the evaluator came to these recommendations and how the recommendations protect the children's best interests.

REPORT SUBMITTED TO THE COURT/
SMITH VS SMITH

RECOMMENDATIONS OF CUSTODY AND VISITATION
OF THE SMITH CHILDREN

RE: SMITH VS SMITH

CASE NO.: CV-2010-0000-DR

DATE: MARCH 20, 2010

1. Joint custody of Sam Smith and Steve Smith be awarded to both parents, Ann Smith and Bob Smith.
2. It is recommended that both children live mostly with their mother, Ann Smith, while visiting regularly with their father, Bob Smith:
    a) Bob would have visitation with Sam on alternate weekends from Friday after school to Monday morning, when he will return him to school. Long weekends during the school year would generally be awarded to Bob. For example, on a 3-day holiday weekend, Bob would have visitation from Friday after school to Tuesday morning, when he returns Sam to school. On teacher in-service weekend, Bob would have visitation from Thursday morning to Monday morning. Additionally, on the alternate week (the week without overnights), Bob would have two evening visits from after school until 7 p.m. The parents can negotiate the days and times for the evening visit. It is

assumed that Bob will be available to care for Sam when he has visitation on the weekends and midweek.

b) Bob would have visitation with Steve on alternate Saturdays from 10 a.m. to 6 p.m. and alternate Sundays from 10 a.m. to 6 p.m. On the alternate week, Steve would be with his father when Sam is with his father for the alternate week evening visits. It is assumed that Bob will be available to care for Steve when he has visitation on the weekend days and during the midweek visits.

c) Summer visitation would remain the same but with the addition of 4 additional overnights with Sam (7 consecutive overnights) twice during the summer months. It is the responsibility of whichever parent is using the extended time to inform the other parent at least 4 weeks before doing so. Furthermore, it is assumed that Bob will be available for child care during the extended times.

d) Summer visitation for Steve would remain the same but with the addition of 3 consecutive overnights twice during the summer months. It is the responsibility of whichever parent is using the extended time to inform the other parent at least 4 weeks before doing so. Furthermore, it is assumed that Bob will be available for child care during the extended visitation time.

e) Holidays can be split or alternated as negotiated by the parents. Christmas day can be split or alternated. The remainder of the Christmas holiday time can be split between the parents for up to 4 consecutive overnights. Spring break would be awarded to Bob for up to 4 consecutive overnights.

f) Regular phone contact needs to be established between the children and their parents. The parents can negotiate the time for this daily contact. Both parents are responsible for facilitating this phone contact.

g) Both parents have the right of first refusal for child care.

h) Travel will be shared equally between the parents.

3. Sam would benefit from regular individual counseling. He is currently seeing a counselor on a biweekly basis. This should continue, perhaps even on a weekly basis. The counselor is encouraged not only to meet with Sam but also to meet with Sam with his father and Sam with his mother. The father–son counseling sessions will help Sam resolve his feelings about the divorce and help him understand that his father loves him and has not replaced him with Linda's children. The mother–son counseling sessions will help Sam separate from his mother more easily and believe that he can be autonomous in his life. Counseling will also help Sam deal with his anxiety and worries about his current life.

4. Sam would benefit from being part of an extracurricular activity such as soccer, tee-ball, or swimming. Sam needs an outlet where he can be a part of a team and see himself as a positive asset to that team. Both parents would be responsible for facilitating his attendance at practice and games.

Both parents would equally share the costs associated with the extracurricular activity.

5. Both parents and the "stepparent" would benefit from parent education/divorce education classes. Potential referrals include the X Counseling Center, the Y Counseling Center, and Z Counseling.

6. Bob would benefit from counseling services to help him better understand any anger issues he may have. Counseling would also help him understand how to be an effective coparent. Possible referrals are ABC Counseling and XYZ Counseling.

7. Ann would also benefit from counseling services to help her learn how to better identify and deal with her emotions concerning the divorce. She will also learn skills that will make her a better coparent. Possible referrals are the XYZ Counseling Center or Dr. Smith (private practice).

8. A regular time each week needs to be established for the parents to communicate with each other about the children. This communication can be over the phone or face-to-face. The parents can negotiate the day and time for this weekly communication opportunity.

9. Because of Steve's age and Sam's emotional immaturity, a shared arrangement at this time is not recommended. A reevaluation should be conducted just before Steve enters kindergarten to determine whether a shared arrangement would then be in the children's best interests. It is hoped that the parents can make any necessary modifications; however, if they are unable to do so, then a formal reevaluation would be necessary and would consider the parents' abilities to communicate effectively and coparent efficiently. A formal reevaluation would also consider both children's best interests and positive growth and development, as well as the parents' current living arrangements.

Evaluator's name, degree, license, certification   DATE

BEFORE THE REPORT IS SUBMITTED TO THE COURT: CONFERENCE CALL

After the recommendations were written, a conference call between the evaluator and the two attorneys was established. This conference call allows the evaluator a chance to tell the attorneys what the recommendations are and answer any questions the attorneys may have about the recommendations. This conference call is an opportunity to clarify, not justify, and to make sure that everyone is on the same page and has the same understanding of the recommendations. After the conference call, hard copies of the recommendations are mailed to each attorney and the court. The attorneys are encouraged to conference by telephone with the evaluator as they try to help the parents develop a parenting plan they can agree on. During the conference call, the evaluator was informed of the court date and put it on the calendar. Most cases settle without going to court, but the evaluator can't count on that happening. The court date was 2 months after the conference call with the attorneys.

AFTER THE REPORT IS SUBMITTED TO THE COURT: PARENT CONTACT

Approximately 1 month before the court date, Ann contacted the evaluator by phone to relate a recent incident involving Sam and his father. Bob cancelled his visitation to go to a funeral with Linda and her children. Sam confided with his mother that he doesn't know why his father does everything for Roy and nothing for him. He told his mother that he hates not only Roy but also his father. While Sam was talking to his mother, he began urinating in his pants. Ann also said that Sam had been having accidents when talking with Bob on the telephone. The following are the notes the evaluator took during the phone conversation:

After the Report Is Submitted to the Court:
Parent Contact Notes

2-19-10   Ann
returned her call

Bob went to CA for funeral
Ann took Sam to school party -
Sam was whiny & finally
told mom that he didn't understand
why dad does everything for
Roy, but not him.
Said he hates Roy & his dad
while he was talking about Roy
he started peeing his pants.

Concerning to Ann - that Bob takes
her child over his own -

Bob wanted to switch days w/ Ann
and she said no - so Bob filed
w/ lawyers about her not co-parenting

Accidents are occurring when Sam
& dad interact over phone - Sam
becomes very anxious and pees pants

The attorneys were unable to help their clients agree to a parenting plan, so the judge ordered them to enter mediation a week before the court date. The mediation looked promising but then broke down, and no resolution was ultimately forthcoming. The evaluator was contacted by Ann's attorney requesting the evaluator's testimony in court about the recommendations provided to the court. Fees for testimony were discussed and the day and time agreed upon.

FINAL CONSIDERATIONS

The evaluator did testify on the date and time set by the court. After the testimony, the evaluator was allowed to leave. The duration of the testimony was noted for billing purposes and was sent to the attorney.

Usually the evaluator will not know how the judge rules in a case. At the beginning of their practice, some evaluators contact the attorneys and ask for feedback about their work in court. Sometimes this is helpful, but sometimes not. It is more helpful if your mentor watches you work on the stand and gives you feedback. If at all possible, try to have this happen at least once.

However, just for a sense of closure in this case, the evaluator contacted one of the attorneys and asked how the judge ruled in this case. The judge's orders followed the recommendations of the evaluator regarding custody and visitation schedule. The judge further ordered that the other recommendations suggested by the evaluator be followed and be included in the parenting plan.

If you are feeling as if this is a long and difficult process, you are correct. But it can also be fascinating and invigorating. Evaluation can be a healing process for parents and children alike. In this case, both parents appreciated being heard and understood even if neither got everything he or she requested from the evaluator when it came to custody and visitation.

Court testimony often puts fear in the heart of the person testifying. Being prepared and understanding what is going to happen will lessen your fear and anxiety. Experience is the best teacher, but in the next chapter we'll look at some guidelines to prepare you to communicate effectively on the witness stand.

10

Court Testimony: Preparation and Appearance

PREPARATION

No one in the world likely looks forward to testifying in court. There are certainly those who make a living testifying and do it often enough that they don't mind testifying, but even those people may not actually look forward to doing so. However, with preparation and practice, testifying in court does not have to be anxiety-producing. Every evaluator and many case managers (but never mediators—all their work is confidential) will have the opportunity to testify in court. Evaluators may testify at least several times a month depending on the number of cases they have, how conflicted the cases are, and what the evaluator's reputation is with the courts and attorneys involved. As a beginning evaluator, you should plan on testifying in at least half your cases. As you become more seasoned and build a reputation as a reasoned and professional evaluator, you will probably testify in only a quarter of your cases. As time goes on and judges and attorneys know you better and develop professional relationships with you, expect to eventually testify in only about 1 in 20 cases. Regardless, at times you will have to testify about your recommendations to the court. This chapter will help you prepare for court testimony. The better prepared you are, the better you will feel about testifying, and the better your testimony will go.

Attorney Consultation Prior to Court

You will be notified to testify about your recommendations by one of the attorneys, generally the attorney representing the client who agrees with your recommendations. Often this notification is done by a simple phone call from the attorney to you; sometimes, however, you will be served with a subpoena. As soon as you are notified, start preparing for court. When you talk to the attorney, find out the date of the testimony and what time you are expected to be called to the stand. Write that down in your calendar. If the date is weeks away, make an appointment to talk with the attorney about the testimony before court. Do not spend time talking about your testimony at the time of the original call. There is always a chance that the case will settle and your testimony will not be necessary, so don't spend your time preparing with the attorney until it seems a certainty that you will testify.

As the time grows near, contact the attorney to verify the court date and that you still need to testify. Sometimes you will find out that the court date has been changed—and everyone knew but you. Don't take it personally: It happens sometimes—put the new date in your calendar and move on. If the date is still correct, verify that the appointment you set up to consult with the attorney is still good. This appointment does not have to be long, nor face-to-face. Plan on talking 15 to 30 minutes by telephone.

Before preparing with the attorney for the testimony, reread your notes and recommendations. Reflect on why you came to the conclusions you did. What compelling reasons led to the recommendations you submitted to the court? As you reread your notes, the case will come back to you in detail. Make notes to yourself about what you think needs to be brought up by the attorney in court to help the judge fully understand your reasoning. This conversation with the attorney is ex parte. It is the only conversation you will have during the case or have about the case that does not take place with both attorneys.

During the conversation, let the attorney know what to ask you during questioning to illuminate the rationale behind your recommendations. Sequence the questions in such a way as to lead the court through your line of reasoning. Be on the same page when it comes to what needs to be asked and brought forth during the court testimony. The attorney will appreciate the input if it will better establish the client's case. But don't presume to tell the attorney how to run his or her case.

It is your job to be collaborative and helpful in establishing to the court that your recommendations are in the best interest of the child. Also ask the attorney what questions might come from the opposing attorney so that you can be prepared to answer them. Remember, the more prepared you feel before testimony, the more comfortable you will be on the stand.

Finally, establish with the attorney when he or she wants you at the court to testify, verifying both the date and the time. The attorney should be able to give you a close approximation of when you will be called to testify. You do not need to come earlier to court, but you must be on time. Remind the attorney that you will be billing his or her office for the cost of the testimony. Tell him or her again what your hourly rate is for testimony and what your travel costs will be (if any). Make a reasonable approximation of what the cost of your testimony will be and suggest that the attorney collect the monies from the client before court so that he or she can pay you in a timely fashion. Your costs start when you walk in the courthouse, whether you are sitting in the corridor outside the courtroom, inside the courtroom, or in the stand. It is to everyone's advantage financially for the attorney to get you on the stand when you arrive at the courthouse and then off the stand as timely as may be.

The attorney may ask whether you need a subpoena in order to testify. If you need a subpoena to get away from work, then ask for the subpoena; if you do not, then assure the attorney that you will be there on the date and at the time agreed upon. At the end of the conversation, provide the attorney with a way to contact you if, for whatever reason, you do not need to go to court. You need to be available in the evening before court, in the early morning before court, and even during the day as the court session is occurring. Often, the case will settle just before beginning, the judge will postpone the hearing, or some other unforeseen event will preclude your testifying. Be sure you are in the loop so that you know not to go to court (wasting your time if you aren't needed) or know that you definitely need to appear.

At the beginning of your testimony, you will be asked about your professional training, licensure, and experience as an evaluator. If you are known to the court, usually both attorneys will agree about your expertise and allow the court to consider you an expert. If you are not known to the court, be prepared to talk about your educational background (giving dates), about how you obtained your training as an evaluator, and about how many cases you have completed as an evaluator.

Often you will be asked to provide a curriculum vitae (CV) to the court. Have a current CV available to hand over to the court to document your professional background and experience. Either create a current CV or dust off an old one—and update it. Do not provide the court an old and noncurrent CV for inspection: This does not enhance your professional credibility.

The night before or the morning of your testimony, review your notes and recommendations once more. If you make notes or an outline to better organize yourself, include this in your case file. Gather your case notes (including a copy of the recommendations) and a copy of your CV and get ready to go to court. You may also want to bring some tissue, some throat lozenges, and reading glasses if you use them.

Going to Court: Professional Dress

Before you go to court, consider what to wear. The court has rules about what court officers can and cannot wear to court. Some jurisdictions are more relaxed than others, but generally men are expected to wear coats and ties and women to dress professionally. What exactly does this mean? For those of you who work in more casual clothes (as is the case for many play therapists) or those of you who wear funky, clingy, or out-of-the-ordinary clothes—you get to go shopping for "court clothes." The court atmosphere is relatively conservative, so you need to look the part of the expert professional and fit into that environment. You don't have to like it; you just have to do it.

Men wear suits or sports jackets, ties, and slacks. There may be courts that allow jeans with a jacket, but they are few and far between. Go buy a well-fitting suit, a dress shirt, and a conservative tie. Buy shoes to match the suit, then shine them. You need to dress at least as well as everyone else in court, and ideally just a little better. You may not like it, and it may not be right, but wearing professional clothes makes others believe that you are in fact the professional you claim to be. Wearing professional clothes can also make you feel more professional, putting you in the correct mindset, ready to testify professionally and with conviction.

Originally, women were expected to wear a conservative suit with a matching skirt. Jewelry and makeup were to be kept to a minimum and hair was to be styled conservatively (for example, in a bun). Today, although women are still expected to wear professional clothes, this can include a suit with a jacket, a matching skirt or pants, and a fairly conservative blouse. Jewelry gets more leeway nowadays, but jewelry that makes noise is generally frowned upon. Hairstyles are left to the woman, but anything too radical (a colored mohawk?) is not encouraged. A female evaluator may like her colored jeans, flowing gypsy skirts, see-through blouses, wedge sandals, bangle bracelets, and flower headband, but the court does not. You may need to purchase clothes that you only ever wear to court—a suit with a matching skirt or pants, a sharp-looking blouse without a lot of frills or patterns, nylons without designs, shoes conservative in both color and style, and jewelry that is not flashy or noisy—and decide on a reasonable hairstyle to go with it. You must match the others in court by your professional dress. You may not like it, but you must look the part of a "court professional." What you look like to others will inform their mindset about your professional abilities as an evaluator. Finally, courtrooms tend to be on the chilly side, so dress warmly if you get cold easily. Asking the judge mid-testimony to turn off the air conditioning is something you should avoid if possible.

So: You are at court at the agreed-upon time, you have reviewed your notes and recommendations, you have familiarized yourself with the case, you have consulted with the attorney who asked you to testify, you are dressed as the professional you are, and you are ready for testimony. Now the "fun" begins.

APPEARANCE

Now comes the moment of your actual testimony. Even evaluators who have testified many times feel a bit nervous and anxious before testifying. However, if you have thoroughly reviewed your notes and understand and can articulate your rationale for making your recommendations, then you are ready to tell the court why you recommended what you did. Before you step up to the witness stand, be aware of some general guidelines for testifying as an expert.

General Guidelines for Testimony

1. You need to be able to explain your work and the rationale behind your recommendations in layman's terms. Do not try to dazzle the court with counseling terms that only you understand—don't end up

explaining terms rather than talking about your recommendations. Avoiding using jargon; instead, use terminology understandable by everyone in the courtroom.

2. Do not go beyond your level of expertise. If you want to impress the court with your infinite wisdom, then you had better have infinite wisdom. Don't attempt to extend your testimony beyond what you yourself did for the court. Being a know-it-all will destroy your credibility with the court.

3. You need to project confidence and conviction and be forthright during your testimony. You are the professional. You were hired by the court to assist the judge in making orders to protect the best interest of the child. To act as if you did not do the best job possible and as if you are not confident in your recommendations does not help the court make the best judgment.

4. Be responsive to any question put to you by either attorney or the judge. Fully answer the question, but do not ramble. Answer completely and succinctly and then stop talking.

5. Do not be an advocate for one party over the other. If you were testifying as one party's counselor, than you would advocate for him or her. But as an evaluator, it is your job to provide information to the court about what you believe is in the child's best interest.

6. In every case there are facts that weigh against your recommendations. You need to be able to admit damaging facts and acknowledge them rather than hedging. For example, if the judge asks you why your recommendations differ from those of the second expert, hired by the opposing side, answer honestly: You don't know. You could make some educated guesses about why, but you don't actually know.

7. Maintain impartiality in both preparation and testimony. Integrity and objectivity are critical factors during the testimony. Don't let a parallel process blind you to seeing both sides of the case. Do not take a stand for one parent and fail to recognize the other parent's redeeming qualities. It is a very rare case in which one parent is totally good and the other parent is totally bad. It is your job to remain impartial in order to provide the best recommendations possible to the court.

8. Do not get angry at the opposing attorney when he or she cross-examines you. Keep your emotions under control. Cross-examination is designed to rattle you, make you backtrack on your

reasoning, and even make you question your abilities and your report. Cross-examination aims to make you emotional, preferably angry, as the attorney tries to discredit your work. But do not become angry. Remain calm, cool, and collected throughout. Your mantra: Nothing will rattle you. The more professional your demeanor during testimony, the more consideration will be afforded your report.

9. Be certain that you know and can talk about the theories and practice of why you did what you did. Understand why you looked for certain factors and how those factors influenced your recommendations. Understand what the opposing side is basing its case on so that you can talk about the pros and cons of that point of view.

10. Always bring your notes of the case, any relevant documents, and a copy of your report with you to court. Never depend on your memory to answer the questions posed by the attorneys or the judge. When you are uncertain about something and need to look at your notes, stop and look at your notes. Do not guess when you can rely on your notes for correct and complete answers.

11. Always remember that you are the court's expert and thus are responsible for maintaining your professionalism at all times. Don't get flustered or lost in the questions or your answers. Be impartial toward both sides, but do not back down from your recommendations unless you are convinced of a compelling reason to do so. Do not take the attorneys' behaviors toward you personally. They are just doing their jobs as advocates for their clients.

Actual Court Testimony

Now that you know and understand the general guidelines, have taken a deep breath, and are determined to remain cool, calm, and collected, the questioning can begin. You are sworn in and you take the stand, notes in hand. The attorney who asked you to testify will begin the questioning. You will be asked questions first to establish your credentials as an expert. After that, questions specific to the case will begin.

Decide where you are going to look or focus your attention as the questions are asked and your answers follow. One of the best ways to avoid being distracted by either the parents or the other attorney is to look at the person asking the questions—and only at that person. Keep your focus on that one person. Eliminate from your view all extraneous factors in the courtroom. By maintaining focus, you are better able to listen to the questions and answer them more completely. Focus, focus, focus.

Every question is important and needs to be answered specifically. The most important thing you need to do while you are testifying is listen to the question, then consider your answer, then talk. Listen to hear what type of question is being asked. Your response needs to specifically answer the question asked by the attorney:

Potential Types of Questions

1. Vague and ambiguous questions.

   If a question seems vague or nonspecific or you don't understand the question, ask to have the question rephrased or its terms defined before answering. Do not answer a question that you don't understand. Do not assume you know what the question means if you are not absolutely sure of the meaning. If you don't understand the question, it is likely that no one else understands the question.

2. Leading questions.

   A leading question is one in which the question's answer is suggested or the witness is simply asked to agree with the question. Be very careful of these types of questions. Only agree with the attorney's answer if you can do so without hesitation or qualifications. If you don't agree with the attorney's suggestion, say so by answering, "No, that is not what I said"; "What I said was . . ."; or "Perhaps I didn't make myself clear; here is what I was saying. . . ." Do not fall for the attorney's attempt to get you to change your testimony and agree to things you don't want to.

3. Compound questions.

   Be very careful of questions that have multiple components. These questions can often confuse you. Before you answer, ask that the question be broken up into separate parts or questions. Answer each part separately and carefully. If the attorney has difficulty separating the parts of the original question, then state that you are going to answer each element one at a time. Don't get caught up in the intricacies of the question. Break it into its parts and answer each part carefully and fully.

4. Hypothetical questions.

These questions are difficult to answer, because the assumptions posed by the attorney may not have anything to do with the case or reality. Your answer should be carefully considered. Answering a hypothetical question often means giving your best guess, so say as much before you answer. "I do not agree with all your assumptions, but assuming that they are accurate, my answer would be . . ." or "My answer to this question is also purely hypothetical."

5. Catch-all questions.

This type of question asks you to reveal the fullness of your knowledge about a particular issue. If you leave some bit of information out, that can be used to trap you in your testimony later. Some catch-all questions, and possible responses, could be as follow:

Q: Tell us all you know about . . .
A: That is all I can think of at this time.
Q: Is that everything that happened?
A: That is all I can remember happening at that time. If you have more specific information that I have not discussed, tell me what it is and I will be more than happy to discuss it.
Q: What is your opinion in this case?
A: One of my opinions is . . .
or
A: If you could specify the particular portion of the case about which you want my opinion, it would be easier for me to respond.

6. Questions pointing out inaccuracies in your testimony.

This type of question is often used by attorneys in an attempt to discredit your answers. If you made a mistake in answering previously or weren't complete in your answer, then say that you wish to correct, clarify, or amplify your answer. You can interrupt at any time and say, "It has occurred to me that I may be able to give a more accurate answer to a question asked earlier, and I'd like to do so now."

7. Yes or no questions.

If you are asked a question that requires a yes or no answer but that needs further explanation, ask permission to give a more complete answer than just a yes or a no. If you aren't given the opportunity to expand your answer, just answer the question; during redirect you will be given the opportunity to give a more complete answer.

8. Paraphrasing questions.

   These questions should put you on alert. They often give the witness a sense of calm rather than the hyperalertness they deserve. Listen very carefully for any subtle changes or inaccuracies in the attorney's paraphrasing before you agree with what he or she says. These questions may begin: "So if I understand correctly, what you are telling me is . . ." or "So let me see if I understand you correctly. . . ." If you don't agree with the paraphrase, then say so and correct the inaccuracy. Just because the attorney says it doesn't mean you have to agree with it.

9. Questions about documents that can be difficult to answer.

   When you are handed a document to consider, look it over carefully before you begin talking about it. If it is a document you haven't seen before, say so and ask for a recess during which you can read it and consider it before answering questions about it. You have already included the documentation you used in making your recommendations; beware of documents that are unfamiliar to you.

10. Questions about conversations or interviews.

    Questions like this need clarification on your part. You need to be specific: Ask whether you are allowed to paraphrase the conversation or should quote exactly what was said during the interview.

11. Questions about the opposing expert or the second opinion report.

    If a question is posed to you about another evaluator's reputation in the field, answer carefully. If you know the expert, say so without gushing about his or her expertise; likewise, don't downplay his or her capabilities. It is best to remain neutral. If you do not have an opinion about the expert's reputation, then say so. You are an expert also, so don't downplay your importance.

12. The question from hell.

    These questions put fear into the heart of anyone who is currently on the witness stand. This question is unanticipated, out of the blue, and takes you completely by surprise. When this type of question comes, take your time before you answer. Take a breath, don't squirm or wring your hands, control your body language, don't look to the other attorney for help (none will be forthcoming!), and think the question through in your mind. Always remember: You are the expert. You know more about this case and why you wrote the recommendations than either attorney or the judge does. You are prepared; you know the details of both sides of this case. You are capable of answering any question posed to you by either attorney. Listen, think, and then answer to the best of your ability.

13. Objection.

Stop talking at once. Let the judge decide how to handle the objection; only then proceed as directed. During testimony, when you hear "Objection!" that means "Stop talking!"

Although some evaluators tell tales of their horrible experiences in court, attorneys and judges are generally respectful of your expertise. They may ask you challenging questions, but that is their job. Your job, then, is to be prepared to answer any question posed to you. Remain as cool and collected as possible during your testimony.

Testimony Demeanor

1. Be professional at all times. Always remember that you are the professional; your judgments and recommendations to the court are important to the successful resolution of the case.

2. Always be courteous and respectful of the attorneys, the judge, and the judicial process.

3. Do not be arrogant, but don't fail to show self-assurance and confidence in your work.

4. Be respectful and courteous to the opposing attorney. This does not mean, however, that you should allow yourself to be backed into a corner by that attorney. Try to never lose your temper regardless.

5. It is not your job to argue with either attorney. You are there to answer questions and communicate why your recommendations are in the child's best interest. Becoming combative with the opposing attorney only makes your position weaker and your recommendations suspect in the court's eyes.

6. Always remember that you are the expert: You did your evaluation with the utmost professionalism. During testimony, sustain your contentions. Just because one side of the case does not like your ultimate conclusions does not mean you should not defend them. What you have written in your report and what you say during

testimony may well be difficult for the parents to hear. That does not mean you should back off from your conclusions just to avoid making the parents uncomfortable. Be consistent and confident—not arrogant—in your demeanor during your testimony, and sustain your conclusions.

After the Testimony

After you have finished testifying, you will be told whether the judge wants you to remain in the courtroom or whether you are released and can leave the building. (Generally, you can go after you complete your testimony.) Be sure to note the time when you step down from the witness stand so that you can bill appropriately for your time. It is generally best to bill the attorney for your time of testimony (and travel time, if appropriate) as soon as you return to the office. Be sure to follow up with the attorney if your bill is not paid in a timely fashion—do not testify for nothing.

DEPOSITIONS

There are times when you will be asked to testify at a deposition. A *deposition* is the same as testifying in court without the judge present. This gives the opposing attorney the opportunity to better understand your position and the reasoning behind your recommendations. Both attorneys are present, but without a judge to rule on objections, the questions asked by the attorneys can be more varied and not based on a foundation. In other words, the attorney can ask questions about whatever he or she wants in order to build his or her case for the actual court testimony. The deposition is conducted at the attorney's office.

What you say in the deposition will come back to haunt you during the court testimony if you aren't consistent. However, this isn't a problem unless you say one thing in the deposition and another during the court testimony. You must remain consistent in your testimony about your work and conclusions. Otherwise, what you said during the deposition will be brought up again in court if your words are significantly different during the court testimony. For example, if during the deposition you testify that the father does not have a relationship with the child and therefore should have limited visitation, but during the court testimony you say that the father has a weak relationship with the child and therefore should have more time with the child to build the relationship, that inconsistency will be a problem in court.

At the conclusion of the deposition, you will be asked whether you want to read the transcript before it becomes official. Always say yes: You want to read the transcript. Then read the transcript page by page and make corrections as directed. You cannot make corrections that change what you said during the deposition because you wish you had said something different. The changes you can make are more to do with the details, such as a mistake in your correct address, and so forth.

Also at the conclusion of the deposition, you will be asked whether you want a copy of the deposition. Always say yes: You want a copy of the deposition. You will reread it before your court testimony to remind yourself of what you said during the deposition. If you find you made an error during the deposition and misspoke, then if it is brought up in court, agree that you realized when rereading the deposition that you misspoke and explain that you want to clarify what you said. If it is not brought up in court, then let it go.

Many evaluators find the deposition more difficult, and perhaps more uncomfortable, than testifying in court. Put yourself in mind as if you are testifying in court. The deposition appears, on the surface, to be more laid back and informal since it is conducted in the attorney's office without the judge. Often the attorneys will dress casually and appear relaxed. You, on the other hand, should appear professional by being dressed and prepared as if you were going to court. Do not be fooled into thinking that the deposition is just a trial run and a practice time for you. The deposition is as important to the case as the actual court trial. After the deposition, bill the attorney who called you to be deposed for your time and travel (if appropriate). The cost of the deposition is the same as the cost for testifying in court.

SECOND OPINION EXPERT

Finally, there will be times during your career when you will be asked to give a second opinion on a case that has been previously evaluated. Many evaluators choose not to be second opinion experts because they do not want to testify against another professional's opinion. Before you accept the second opinion expert role, find out some specifics from the attorney.

When the attorney contacts you hoping that you will become his or her side's expert, make it very clear that you will not find for one side or the other but rather work for the child and his or her best interest. There are experts who are hired for their second expert opinion in the knowledge that they will always find for the side that hired them. Do not become one of those people. Even as a second opinion, remain unbiased and speak for the child's best interest regardless of who hired you. Be very clear to the attorney that this is your stance. Tell the attorney what you need to do to come to reasoned conclusions and how much it will cost. The second opinion expert generally does an evaluation just as if he or she were the first evaluator, but he or she does have the first evaluator's report and recommendations to consider in his or her conclusions. The attorney will ask you to not write a report until you have consulted with him or her about your potential recommendations: If your report is not favorable to his or her side, he or she will pay you for your services and say thank you. If your report is favorable to his or her side, he or she will ask you to write the report and submit it either to him or her or to the court. You should have already been paid for your services at this point. If not, bill for your time now.

When there are two experts testifying in court, it can turn into a fight between the experts about what is in the child's best interest. Your job as the second expert is to testify about your recommendations and conclusions just as you would if you were the only evaluator. Additionally, you will be asked to explain why your recommendations are different from the first evaluator's.

The same rules apply for testimony, except it is easier as the second opinion to become defensive and emotional during testimony. Avoid doing so at all costs. Your opinion is your opinion, and you came to it through professionalism and reasoned thought. There will be areas in which you will agree with the original evaluator; acknowledge those areas if they are brought up during questioning. The areas in which you don't agree will more than likely be many and will certainly be brought up. Clearly defend your position and how you reached your conclusions. Do not speculate about how the other evaluator could have made the recommmendations he or she made unless it is clear why he or she did. Speculation is just that. Let the other evaluator defend and communicate his or her position. However, beware of portraying yourself during testimony as all-knowing and "right" and the other evaluator as an incompetent fool. He or she may be, but it is not your job to continually point that out. The court will draw its own conclusions after hearing testimony from both experts.

When you are through testifying, ask to be released by the judge so that you can leave the building; note the time so that you can bill for your time testifying, and go about your day. When you get back to your office, bill the attorney immediately. Be sure to get paid in a timely fashion for your work.

Testifying in court may never be what you would consider fun, but it does not have to be torture, either. It's all about being prepared and being able to communicate with others clearly and understandably. The more often you testify, the more familiar you will become with the process and thus the more comfortable you will feel. However, do not become so comfortable that you fail to prepare completely for court, or you will be caught flat-footed by an attorney who was just waiting for you to slip up.

There is actually something exhilarating about testifying well in court. You will always think "I wish I had said that" or "I wish I had not said that," but that's just human nature. Don't dwell on what you wish would have happened, but rather on how you testified overall. Think of court testimony as just another adventure in your professional career.

11

Final Thoughts

You have now learned about the basics of working successfully in the family courts. Becoming a custody evaluator, mediator, or case manager is not for the faint of heart. But the challenge makes this work interesting and fulfilling. These jobs require that you use your counseling skills not as a therapist, but rather as an impartial advocate in the court system for a child and his or her best interest. You are often the only person who truly speaks for the child in what is usually the most difficult time in his or her life. As a mediator, case manager, and particularly custody evaluator, you can significantly influence how the child's future unfolds, as well as the parents'.

Even so, you are not going to make everyone happy; this is often one of the hardest parts for a counselor to accept. The ultimate goal of a therapist is to help his or her clients feel more positive and happy in their lives. But that doesn't usually happen in family court. Often one party to the case will not feel positive about the conclusions of your work—that's the nature of the work. Nonetheless, you can do certain things to help both parents and children in this journey through and beyond divorce. Establishing opportunities for parents and children to learn and talk about this journey is one way to lessen the collateral damage.

The court system is always looking for ways to eliminate recycled cases. The courts want as few modifications of a divorce decree as possible. They want parents to work together as effective coparents to raise the healthiest children possible. If the parents learn to coexist with each other in at least a functional way, they can then agree to necessary modifications as the child ages and circumstances change. Ideally, the parents can make the decisions for their child rather than having the court system do it. Many jurisdictions are instituting classes to help parents and children better understand the effects of divorce on their lives both in the present and in the future. As a professional mental health provider, you can help the court establish these classes and other such opportunities.

PARENTING CLASSES FOR DIVORCED PARENTS

One class that is benefiting parents in many jurisdictions occurs simultaneously with a filing for divorce if there are children involved. The class is taught generally in the evening and lasts approximately 3 hours. Generally, there is only one session, and the parents are required to attend it before the judge makes any order to dissolve the family. One class barely scratches the surface of all the parents need to know about the effects of a divorce, but one class is better than none. This class is taught by a professional counselor who is fluent in the realities of the effects of divorce on children. Some places that have access to a university counseling department use graduate students to teach the classes under supervision by a counseling faculty member. This is a great opportunity for the students to practice their communication skills and work in a real situation with real clients.

The class is generally taught in a classroom in the courthouse. Because of potential problems arising from emotional adults attending the class, at least one court marshal is assigned to each class. If a restraining order or no contact order is in effect, the parents are assigned to different classes. Depending on the situation in that particular jurisdiction, there may also be a police standby assigned to the parking lot before the class and at the conclusion of the class to discourage arguments in the parking lot between parents.

The classes cover a variety of topics, all dealing with how children are affected by a divorce in their family. Topics generally include the myths and truths about the effects of a divorce, what a child experiences as his or her parents embark on a divorce, and how the parents can reduce the amount of anguish the child experiences through this process. This class provides the parents with the truth about what they are doing to their child and how they can reduce the collateral damage done to the child now and into the future. This is not an opportunity for parents to air their tales of woe, but rather a chance to teach them how to make the divorce as easy on their child as possible.

Some of the class is also spent discussing what the parents are going through as the divorce proceeding moves along. Discovering that others are feeling the same as they are, having their own rollercoasters of emotions, is helpful for the parents. The children are suffering, but so are the parents. Change is never easy, and change fraught with emotions and concerns is particularly difficult. The class provides the parents with ways to deal with their emotions both when they are alone and when they have to deal with their soon-to-be ex-spouse.

Part of the class focuses on how to become an effective coparent. Coparenting skills need to be practiced and developed over time to reach effectiveness; even so, the class does provide the groundwork necessary for the parents to begin the process. Many parents do not even have a concept of how to coparent, and they need help to become coparenting adults.

Additionally, this class teaches the parents the process that will occur within the family court, from filing for the divorce through the final orders the judge will sign concluding the case. The class will provide information about child support, costs associated with obtaining a divorce, and other financial matters. For those parents proceeding as pro se litigants, paralegals are available at the conclusion of the class to help them file the required documents. This class does not provide legal advice, but it does give direction toward better understanding court procedures.

The parents are asked to evaluate the class at the end. What little data is available seems to show that parents believe these classes are helpful to them. The parents report that they learned new information, left better understanding what to expect, and were glad they attended. Although many parents said they resented having to attend the class, in the end they were glad the court required their attendance.

CHILDREN'S CLASS

Another class often provided by the courts is a class for children whose parents are divorcing. Because this type of class has to be divided up into several different classes to accommodate the different developmental levels of the children, it is more difficult to establish. However, even though it may be more difficult to set up, it is often the most beneficial thing that happens for children caught in the divorce process.

The classes are often taught when the parents are attending their class. Most jurisdictions strongly encourage the parents to enroll their child in this class. The parents are given information about the class so that they understand that this is not child care, nor is it traditional group therapy. It is a class that helps children understand why they are feeling what they are feeling, that others are feeling the same way, that the responsibility of the divorce is not theirs, and that things will get better (or at least more normal) as time goes on. In addition to teaching, this class also allows the children to talk about what is going on in their lives because of and in spite of the divorce. For many children, this will be their one and only opportunity to talk about their feelings and understand that there are other children who are feeling the same way.

These classes have to be taught by professionals who work with children therapeutically in their practice. The selection of the "teachers" needs careful consideration. Again, graduate counseling students made available through a university counseling department can gain valuable clinical hours under careful supervision by a faculty member. Although there can be one primary lesson plan for all the different classes, each class needs to be developmentally appropriate for the children attending it. In other words, each class may want to discuss what is happening between the members' parents, but that topic has to be approached differently for the 5- to 8-year-olds versus the 13- to 16-year-olds.

The initial setup of the children's classes is time-consuming and difficult. However, after they are established and staffed and their bugs have been worked out, they become one of the best things the court can do for these children. If the court works for the best interests of the child, then establishing this type of class for them is doing just that. The victims of a divorce are the children; thus, they both need and deserve services that will at least minimize their victimization.

You cannot be an instructor in parents' or children's classes. If you want to be an evaluator, mediator, or case manager, you must maintain the boundaries necessary to work in those areas. However, you can help establish these classes and advocate for them with the family court. You can also develop curriculum and assist in hiring the right people for the classes. But you cannot one night be in front of the parents' class teaching them and the next day have them in your office for an evaluation. Decide which you want to do.

DIVORCE EDUCATION CLASSES/PARENTS

Although you cannot be an instructor in a parents' or children's class, you can develop some other group classes within your practice that you can lead while also being an evaluator, mediator, or case manager. These group classes are not established by the court but can be used as referral sources both by the court and by other practitioners. Three types of groups can be established within your practice: divorce education classes for parents, stepparenting education classes, and divorce groups for children. These groups are few and far between in the therapeutic world but could be very useful to their participants, as well as money-making for your practice.

Divorce education classes are really more like psychoeducational groups for parents who have divorced and who want to learn how to be better coparents for their children. This is not parent education, but rather education focusing on parenting children in a divorce situation. The classes can be set up however you choose, both in terms of scheduling and fees. This addition to your practice might well be beneficial to your bottom line.

Initially, it will take time to establish the outline and objectives for the classes. Topics might include working with the ex-spouse from a business proposition rather than an emotional stance, talking about what emotions the parent is still carrying from the divorce, recognizing how this emotional baggage plays a role in communicating effectively with the ex-spouse, recognizing triggers for emotional outbursts, knowing when to talk and when to not talk, being able to speak as an adult in a businesslike manner, and so forth.

A second class might focus on what coparenting is and is not. Teaching parents how to be effective coparents and warning them about pitfalls is very helpful to divorced parents. Some parents stumble across skills that work with their ex-spouse and parenting their children. However, most parents never find their way to that skill set. Understanding what coparenting is as well as what its skills are and how to effectively use them mostly benefits the children but also helps the court system by reducing the number of high-conflict modification cases.

A third class might be role-playing and practicing the skills the participants learned in the first two classes. Developing role-play situations allows parents to practice using these skills to promote good coparenting for their children into the future.

DIVORCE EDUCATION CLASSES/STEPPARENTS

The second type of class you might consider establishing in your practice is a class for stepparents. Again, you could establish an outline and goals for the class, including what stepparenting is and is not. You could teach skills to the stepparents that would be helpful in establishing a relationship with the stepchild and the ex-spouse. The classes would teach the stepparent what his or her responsibilities are in dealing with his or her stepchild as well as the child's parents' responsibilities.

You could also discuss how to avoid becoming the catalyst for conflict between the parents and instead be viewed as an adult concerned about the child's best interest. It is a hard road to walk for the stepparent to be loyal and supportive for his or her new spouse while understanding the importance of the role of the ex-spouse. Blended families need to be considered as well. Teaching how to establish a blended family that is mostly functional would be a great benefit not only to the children but also to all the adults involved in these new families.

DIVORCE EDUCATION CLASSES/CHILDREN

The last area you could consider adding to your practice is a divorce group therapy/class for children. Children always benefit from being a member of a group that not only teaches about the effects of being a child of divorce but also lets each child talk about his or her feelings and experiences related to the breakup of his or her family. In many schools, if the school counselor is doing his or her job, divorce groups will be available. Sometimes these are called "friendship groups"; but regardless, they provide an opportunity for the child to find ways to cope with his or her new life. If the groups are available through the school, then that is a good referral source for the courts; if not, then your practice would become the referral source for the courts.

These groups must be set up with the developmental needs of the child in mind. The basic outline and goals for the groups are constant over all the different age groups, but the road map to achieving the goals is different. If you are not prepared to work successfully with young children, perhaps you could involve another colleague who is. If you work successfully with adolescents and have a colleague who works best with younger children, then join forces in setting up these divorce groups.

Topics you might consider for these groups include what emotions are, what emotions you are dealing with currently, how you feel when you are around your parents and stepparents, and what it feels like when your parents don't get along with each other or when they talk poorly about each other. Finding out that others feel the same as he or she does is healing for a child. Knowing that there are others dealing with the same type of experiences allows the child to not feel alone.

The groups also must focus on coping skills for the child, finding ways of letting the feelings out that are functional rather than dysfunctional, reducing stress, and knowing when to speak and take responsibility and when to be quiet. The groups need to teach the children how to protect themselves and how to be happy in their new life. Sometimes the best groups are those that just follow the needs of their members. So it will be with these groups.

After the groups and classes are established and are given positive feedback from the participants, the attorneys, the court, and other evaluators, then mediators and case managers will make referrals to your practice. There will always be parents and children who are going through divorce and who need help. Since this is a therapy group, many insurance providers will pay for your services. There is money to be made in providing these services.

CONCLUSION

That's it. I hope this book has inspired you to at least consider becoming involved with the family court system. You might want to be involved on the front lines of high-conflict cases as an evaluator, as the person who is trying to keep the lid on cases and resolve them through mediation, or as the person who is trying to negotiate peace between the warring parties by serving as the case manager. You may want to lead classes and groups teaching parents and children how to cope successfully within a divorce situation, thus eliminating problems before they arise or become explosive. Whatever role you choose to take, you will find a challenge and a sense of accomplishment not often found in the other areas of professional mental health practice.

BIBLIOGRAPHY

Arizona Supreme Court, Court Services Division, Family Law Unit. (2001). *Model parenting time plans for parent/child access.*

Association of Family and Conciliation Courts. (2006). *Planning for shared parenting: A guide for parents living apart.* Fort Lauderdale, FL: Author.

Association of Family and Conciliation Courts. (2013). Retrieved from http://afccnet.org/About/AboutAFCC

Ball, S., MA; DAPA; CASA of the Pike's Peak Region. (2004). *Recommendations for supervised parenting time: How much, how often?*

Baris, M., & Garrity, C. (1998). *Children of divorce: A developmental approach to residence and visitation.* Powder Springs, GA: Blue Ridge Printing Company.

Common Legal Terms Explained. (2013). Retrieved from http://www.ncsmc.org.au/wsas/legal_terms_explained.htm

Dial, L., & May, C. (1989). *Expert testimony.*

Forensic Psychology. (n.d.). Retrieved from http://en.wikipedia.org/wiki/Forensic_psychology

State of Idaho, Idaho Rules of Civil Procedure Rule 16(q). (2013). *Parenting time evaluation.*

State of Idaho, Idaho Statutes Title 32, Chapter 7, # 32-717. (1995). *Custody of children: Best interests.* Boise, ID: Idaho State Supreme Court.

State of Idaho, Sixth Judicial District. (2009). *Family Court Services parent resource booklet.*

State of Idaho, Third Judicial District. (2008). *Focus on children: Parenting apart education.* Caldwell, ID.

State of Oregon, Oregon Judicial Department. (2009). *Long distance schedule.* Retrieved from http://courts.oregon.gov/OJD/docs/OSCA/cpsd/courtimprovement/familylaw/Attachment4A-LongDistanceScheduletabtest2savablefinal8-08.pdf

State of Oregon, Oregon Judicial Department. (2009). *Medium distance schedule*. Retrieved from http://courts.oregon.gov/OJD/docs?OSCA/cpsd/courtimprovement/familylaw/Attachment 4A-MediumDistanceScheduletabtest2savableFinal.pdf

State of Oregon, Oregon Judicial Department. (2009). *Sample parenting schedules*. Retrieved from http://courts.oregon.gov/OJD/docs/OSCA/cpsd/courtimprovement/familylaw/AllSampleSchedules-WhatIsBestForMyChild.pdf

State of Washington, Spokane County Superior Court. *Child-centered residential schedules*. Spokane, WA: Washington Superior Court.

INDEX